WWW.ZONDERVAN.COM

ZONDERVAN™

invert

Secret Power for Girls
Identity, Security, and Self-Respect in Troubling Times

Susie Shellenberger

Secret Power for Girls: Identity, Security, and Self-Respect in Troubling Times

Copyright © 2003 by Youth Specialties

Youth Specialties Books, 300 South Pierce Street, El Cajon, CA 92020, are published by Zondervan, 5300 Patterson Avenue SE, Grand Rapids, MI 49530

Library of Congress Cataloging-in-Publication Data

Shellenberger, Susie.
    Secret power for girls : identity, security, and self-respect in
troubling times / Susie Shellenberger.
       p. cm.
    Summary: Discussion, questions and answers, illustrations, diary
excerpts, and real-life examples provide a "map" for using the Bible and
daily prayer to achieve self-esteem and self-confidence.
    ISBN 0-310-24972-4
    1.   Teenage girls--Religious life--Juvenile literature. 2.   Teenage
girls--Conduct of life--Juvenile literature. 3.   Self-esteem in
adolescence--Religious aspects--Christianity--Juvenile literature. 4.
Christian life--Biblical teaching--Juvenile literature. [1. Teenage
girls--Conduct of life. 2. Self-esteem--Religious aspects--Christianity.
3. Christian life.] I. Title.
    BV4551.3.S545 2003
    248.8'33--dc21
                                                         2003005326

Web site addresses listed in this book were current at the time of publication. Please contact Youth
Specialties via e-mail (YS.YouthSpecialties.com) to report URLs that are no longer operational and replacement URLs if available.

Portions of this book might be appropriate for more mature readers. There are occasional discussions of rape,
drugs, etc.

Edited by Rick Marschall and Laura Gross

Proofed by Michael Ribas

Cover and interior design by Proxy Design

Printed in the United States of America

08 09 10 11 12 • 10 9 8

1	Hey, I Want That!	6
2	Emily Knows the Secret!	14
3	Plugging Into the Secret	20
4	Discovering More of the Secret	28
5	Growing Strong in the Secret	36
6	Growing Stronger in the Secret	44
7	Understanding the Truth	52
8	Plug Into the Power (Part 1)	62
9	Plug Into the Power (Part 2)	70
10	Sad Beginning…Happy Ending	78
11	What Are the Gifts?	84
12	The Fruit of the Spirit	90
13	What's Your Gift?	102
14	Discovery Sometimes Takes a While	116
15	Counterfeit Power	124
16	Deceit from the Enemy	134
17	Secret Power Girls Are Overcomers	140
18	Living It Out	150
19	Questions and Answers	162
20	Calling All Secret Power Girls!	168

Hey, I Want That!

1

Fifteen-year-old Ashley slammed the front door of her house, threw her backpack on the floor, bolted upstairs, and shut her bedroom door.

"Ugh!" she screamed as she grabbed her journal and stretched across her bed.

Using her favorite green gel pen, she wasted no time putting her thoughts on paper.

I'm such a loser. I hate it! I've wanted Jeremy to notice me for two weeks, and today he finally got close enough to catch my eye in the cafeteria. Well, I got nervous and bumped into the kid in front of me. He made me drop my entire tray! It was so stupid! Everyone laughed. And then they all started clapping. I never wanna go back to school again. Jeremy must think I'm the most uncoordinated person in the world! How come I can't do anything right?

+ + + + + + + + + + + + + + + + +

Natasha unloaded her backpack on the couch, grabbed a couple of cookies, and settled into the oversized chair in the living room. It was her favorite place to unwind. Even though the chair was old, frayed, and a little lumpy, Natasha enjoyed snuggling against the soft, worn fabric.

After carefully balancing her diary on her knees and placing the last cookie on the arm of the chair, she began her entry for the day.

Whew! I don't think I've ever had a day like this. Totally unbelievable. I mean, my life could definitely be the next TV sitcom!

I'll start at the beginning. Not because I wanna relive it, but because if I don't get it down in writing, someday my grandkids will never believe me. Well, here it is—Natasha's documented proof!

Okay, my alarm didn't go off because I had mistakenly set it for 6 p.m. instead of 6 a.m. (This should have been my first clue that my brain was in the freezer with last night's ice cream.)

As I was drying my hair, the blow-dryer broke. Yep, that's right: the only blow dryer in the house! So I had to go to school with wet hair. And wouldn't you know it, the hot new guy—the one I've been dying to meet—walked right in front of me and made eye contact. I was so nervous—I dropped my science project. He stopped to pick it up and said, "Hi, I'm Dominik." And all I could do was smile and say, "Dominik, even though first period hasn't even started yet, it's already been a really long day for me. Just call me W.H.—short for Wet Head."

Then I ran to class, but the bell rang before I could get there, so naturally I got a tardy. "That's your third tardy, Natasha," Mr. Mathers said. "I'll see you in detention today after school."

Even though I hate sitting in detention, it gives me a chance to get my homework done before I leave school. And (this may sound lame) I really enjoy meeting the other kids who are stuck in detention with me. Sometimes I pull my Bible outta my backpack and just set it on my desk while I'm doing homework. You'd be surprised how many kids ask about it!

You'd think things would get better as the day progressed, wouldn't you? Not a chance! This is my life, remember, Diary? I just had to laugh.

We had a fire drill between third and fourth periods, and I tripped going down the stairs. Mrs. Hoskins sent me to the nurse, who wrapped my ankle in one of those beige ace bandages (it totally clashed with the orange shirt I was wearing).

Okay, my hair's still not dry. I have an ace bandage around my ankle, I've got detention coming up, I'm limping through the halls, and when I finally get my lunch and sit down to eat it in the cafeteria, I totally miss the chair and land right on my bottom.

The entire caf is clapping and laughing. So I stand, take my bow, and hit the side of my milk carton with a fork before beginning my acceptance speech: "Thank you very much! I especially wanna thank the Academy of Cafeteria Workers, the Academy of Higher Learning, and those who'll be in detention with me after school today."

Everyone was dying laughing—including me—what could I do but laugh? And when you think about it, it really was funny. I looked hideous! I now had baked beans on my orange shirt (they splattered all over my chest when I missed my chair and

tipped the edge of my tray) and the remains of a barbecued pork sandwich on my lap.

During fifth period I gave my science report and displayed my homemade map of North America with its rivers, hills, mountains, ravines, and national parks. I tried to explain why the Rocky Mountains weren't so rocky after I dropped the map in the hall this morning before school. I laughed as I picked a few "new items" (leftovers from the accident) off of Colorado—a paper clip, a broken press-on nail, and a huge dust ball. "Scientists have recently discovered these items growing and reproducing at an alarming rate in the Colorado Rockies," I said.

The whole class was laughing, including Mrs. Rawlings. Afterward, she told me she appreciated my sense of humor. Well, that's nice to know, but it doesn't make up for the C she gave me, now does it?

With school finally over, I felt a little relief as I headed to my locker to get my stuff for detention. I know this will be hard to believe, but after I got out my books and stuff, I slammed the sleeve of my shirt in the locker door. Yep, the sleeve of my favorite orange shirt—which is now orange and brown, thanks to the cafeteria incident—ripped.

I limped into detention with my ace bandage unraveling, my torn and stained shirt stinking like picnic food, and my hair sagging toward my shoulders. In spite of my bedraggled appearance, I was grateful for the chance to get started on my homework. I'd probably been into it for five minutes when I heard a voice behind me say, "Hi, W.H."

I looked around ... and yes, it was him—Dominik!

"Well, I'm not a wet head anymore," I said. "My hair finally dried in a nice matted sort of way. I'm trying to go for one of those celebrity styles you only see in magazines."

He laughed.

I laughed. (My heart raced.)

"I'm new here," he finally said.

"I know."

"Great performance today in the caf."

"Oh, no. You saw that, too?"

"So when's the encore?"

I laughed. "I'd like to say never, but knowing my luck, you'll probably catch a few more performances before the end of the week."

He laughed, and his eyes twinkled slightly.

"Most girls I know would've been devastated if they'd had a day like yours. But you...you're different. What's your name—your real name?"

"Natasha."

"So what's your secret, Natasha?" he asked.

And I smiled remembering the Bible I'd put in my backpack this morning.

+ + + + + + + + + + + + + + + + + +

Hey, what's the deal? It doesn't take a rocket scientist to figure out that Natasha had a way more terrible day than Ashley. But while Ashley came home angry and depressed, Natasha can't wait to share the day with her future grandkids!

Glad you asked. It almost seems like Natasha has some kind of secret, doesn't it?

Yeah! A major secret. And not only that...but it's like she has some kind of power or something that enables her to turn a bad day into a good one. What gives?

You're right. Natasha *does* have a secret. She also has a special power. And not only does that power help her turn bad days into good ones, it also helps Natasha like herself in spite of her outer appearance, find the humor in embarrassing situations, and feel confident enough to reach out to those around her.

So what's the secret? And where I can get this special power?

You're already on track! You're in the right place at the right time. And you're holding the map—this book—that will answer those questions.

Great! So let's keep going.

Wait a sec. This book is so important and holds such incredible truths that you'll want to soak in each page. The information printed in the next few chapters is more valuable than anything you'll ever read. So pause for a second. Take a deep breath. And let's pray.

Pray?

Yes, pray.

I've never prayed before reading any other books.

This isn't like any of your other books. And you want to get it, don't you? Really get it? Understand it? Make the secret power not just something you read about but something that actually becomes part of your life?

Well, yeah.

Okay, then. We need to pray. It's that important. I'll make

it easy—I'll write the prayer below and you pray it.

All right.

> *Dear Jesus:*
>
> *I gotta admit, it feels kind of weird praying about a book. But I understand that what's inside is really important—so important it could change my life forever. I'd like that, Jesus. I really would. It's easy for me to get down on myself. I want to know the secret of loving me like You do. And if there really is some kind of special power that could help me be a better person and make me confident—well, I want it!*
>
> *So, please Jesus, help me understand what's inside this book. I really do wanna get it. Help me not just read it; help me soak it up and live it. In Your name I pray, Amen.*

It's also important that you enjoy this book. So let's grab a few things to make the journey fun, okay? I'm gonna get a Coke, because that's my favorite drink. You get your fave drink, maybe a few munchies, and a pen.

I like the drink and munchies part, but why do I need a pen? This isn't going to be like school, is it?

No. You won't get detention if you don't have a pen. But if you do have a pen, you can actually participate inside the book. Sort of an interactive thing. Not only that, but you can use your pen to mark things you want to remember so you can go back and read them again later. So grab your drink, your munchies, and your favorite pen. Then meet me here in five minutes, okay? I'll wait for you. In fact, while you're gone, I'll just sit here and doodle.

Emily Knows the Secret!

Okay, I've got my drink, my munchies, and my favorite pen. So what's the secret?

Before we get into the facts, let's take a peek at a real-life gal who knows the secret and has the special power.

Meet 19-year-old Emily Copeland from Denver, Colorado. She needs a lot to have fun—a lot of water, that is! Emily is a professional wakeboarder. If you're wondering what's involved with this sport, think water-skiing—then think again.

If you've ever been water-skiing, you already know about the wake—that strong wave of water between you and the boat. If you're an *adventurous* skier, you sometimes jump the wake, ride the wake, or pop the wake. It all involves water and skill. If you're a *wimpy* skier (like me), you cross the wake—but completely by accident while screaming and praying simultaneously.

Emily's *in love* with the wake. In other words, she crosses it, jumps it, and rides it—on purpose! And that's what wakeboarding is—using the wake to do your tricks.

Okay, this is where your pen comes in. (Remember, I said this book was going to be interactive? Well, now's your chance!) Grab your pen and take this quiz. No, we're not playing school—but I wanna make sure you're still with me! Just circle the letter next to each of the correct responses on the next page.

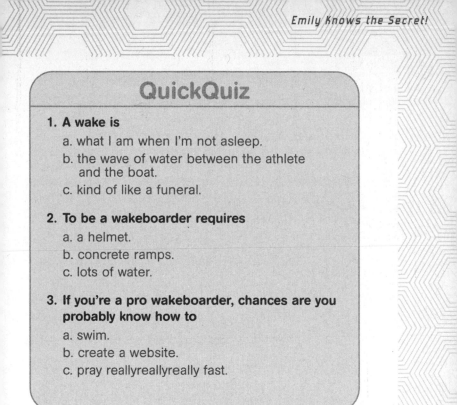

QuickQuiz

1. A wake is
   a. what I am when I'm not asleep.
   b. the wave of water between the athlete and the boat.
   c. kind of like a funeral.

2. To be a wakeboarder requires
   a. a helmet.
   b. concrete ramps.
   c. lots of water.

3. If you're a pro wakeboarder, chances are you probably know how to
   a. swim.
   b. create a website.
   c. pray reallyreallyreally fast.

Okay, now that I know you're still with me, let's learn more about Emily and wakeboarding. To get a feel for what it's like to ride on water, imagine pedaling your bicycle off a ramp—only your "bike" is a sleek board with fins that help you steer and your "ramp" is a strong ripple of water between you and the boat that's pulling you.

If your timing is right, you can jump 20 feet into the air by crossing over the wake. And when you cross *back*— again, it's timing. If you were ranked first in the junior women's division when you were just 15, like Emily was, you could catch another 20 feet of air! Back and forth. Back and forth. And if you decided to turn pro, like Emily has, you could do a 360—a complete turn in the air!

Sometimes Emily lands on the water really hard, which means major pain on her knees and back. And she doesn't win every competition she enters. So how does she maintain her positive attitude and love for life during the tough times?

Emily has a secret.

She has a personal, growing relationship with the Creator of the universe. In other words, she knows God—personally! He makes her smile. He gives her strength. He provides the guidance she needs. And it really does make all the difference in the world.

"It helps so much to know that I can always talk to Him," she says. "He's always there to hold me, pick me up, and see me through the hard times."

Emily tuned in to the secret of knowing Christ when she was only three years old. "I became a Christian when I first understood the gospel," she says. Ever since I was three, my goal has been to keep growing closer and closer to God."

Emily is so serious about her relationship with God and sharing it with others, she's started a chapel service for other professional wakeboarders on tour.

But Emily's faith doesn't end with water and a fun tour with other pros. During her spare time you'll find her serving meals with her family at a mission in downtown Denver. "God wants us to be servants," she says. "It's easy to serve Him when you're in the spotlight and winning titles and competitions, but I want to give Him just as much when the cameras aren't around and no one's applauding."

> Secret: Something kept hidden or unexplained; mystery.

+ + + + + + + + + + + + + + + + + + +

Did you catch Emily's secret? It's the same secret Natasha (from Chapter 1) has.

Hey, wait a sec! I've heard secrets are bad.

That's true. Secrets that are dangerous, exclude others, or are in disobedience to authority are bad. But this book is all about a secret that's GOOD. The secret is **Jesus Christ**.

Check this out: "We speak of God's secret wisdom, a wisdom that has been hidden and that God destined for

our glory before time began. None of the rulers of this age understood it" (1 Corinthians 2:7-8 *NIV*).

Wow! You're invited to tap into a secret that even the world's leaders don't understand! And before time began, God dreamt of sharing this secret with *you*. You must be pretty important. Do you realize that? How special does that make you feel?

Okay, it's time to use your pen again. In the space provided jot down how it makes you feel to know the God of the universe wants to share His personal secret with you.

Check out the same verse in another translation: "The wisdom I proclaim is God's secret wisdom, which is hidden from human beings, but which he had already cho-

_____

_____

_____

_____

_____

_____

_____

_____

_____

_____

sen for our glory even before the world was made. None of the rulers of this world knew this wisdom" (1 Corinthians 2:7-8 *Good News Bible*).

Take a moment to *paraphrase* the above verses (put them into your own words). (Aren't you glad you have that pen? It would be sooooo boring to just read this book, huh?) Oh, and while you're putting the Scripture into your own words, go ahead and insert your own

_____'s **Paraphrase of 1 Corinthians 2:7-8**
(write your name here)

_____

_____

_____

_____

_____

_____

_____

_____

_____

_____

_____

_____

_____

_____

_____

name in it. After all, God was talking to *you* when He breathed that verse into being!

Do you understand the beginning of the secret? Natasha's and Emily's secret is they each have a strong, personal relationship with Jesus Christ. God wants *you* to participate in this secret as well! He wants you to get to know Him on a first-name basis. And when you do, you'll begin to tap into all that is strong and good and mighty and pure. In other words, you'll be tapping into all that God is! But we'll get to that later.

First things first.

Plugging Into the Secret

3

First things first.

You already said that. It was the last sentence of chapter 2.

Glad you're paying attention. I said it again because it's worth repeating. You know, kind of like when your teacher says the same thing over and over again?

Wait a sec! You said this wasn't going to be like school.

You're right. Go grab a refill on your drink. See, you can't do that at school!

Okay, but this time I'm changing from a Coke to lemonade. Now keep going. I'm just starting to get into this.

Okay. First things first.

You said that already.

Just stick with me. When you write a book, I'll read all the stuff you wanna repeat, okay?

Deal.

First things first: Do you have a relationship with Jesus Christ?

Sure. I go to church.

Yeah, but do you know Him personally?

I have a Bible.

But do you know God like your best friend?

Whoa! I'm not sure that's possible. After all we are talking about GOD, right?

Right.

I'm not sure anyone really knows GOD.

Yes, many do. And you can, too, through His Son, Jesus Christ.

Yeah, I know a lot about Jesus.

But there's a difference in knowing *about* Jesus and in knowing Him *personally*. You see, when you establish a personal, growing relationship with Jesus Christ, you're

getting to know God. Jesus Christ is the bridge to God.

And knowing Jesus is the secret to being like Emily and Natasha?

Yes. Well, kind of. I mean getting to know Jesus won't turn you into a professional wakeboarder, but it will put you on the road to discovering the special power you need to be confident, to love yourself, and to tap into some incredible gifts from God!

Okay, I'll be honest. I don't really know if I have a personal relationship with Christ.

And that's exactly where God wants you to begin—with total honesty. Pull out your pen again. Let's take a quick yes-or-no quiz that will help determine if you have a relationship with Christ, okay?

QuickQuiz

1 **Have you ever admitted to Christ that you're a sinner?**

Yes   No

2 **Have you ever asked Christ to forgive your sins?**

Yes   No

3 **Have you accepted His forgiveness for your sins?**

Yes   No

4 **Are you seeking to obey Him?**

Yes   No

5 **Do you know for sure that you'd go to heaven if you died tonight?**

Yes   No

If you answered no to the above questions, you don't have a personal relationship with Christ. But the good news is that God invites you—through His Son, Jesus Christ—to establish an eternal (as in forever and ever and ever) relationship with Him, your Maker.

Okay. I want that. I want in on the secret of who God is and all He has to offer. And I understand now that I need a personal relationship with Jesus Christ to make that happen. So how do I establish and maintain a relationship with Jesus?

By following a series of steps.

Prayer. Eternal life is a gift from God. There's nothing you can do to earn His favor. You can't buy His forgiveness, you can't sneak into heaven when He's not watching, and you'll never be good enough to become a Christian. It's God's gift to you simply because He loves you. In fact, He's crazy about you! You probably already know that He loves you so much He sent His only Son, Jesus Christ, to die for you.

Yeah, I've heard that a lot. But I've never understood it. Why'd Jesus have to die for my sins? I don't get that.

God is perfect, and His kingdom is perfect. Therefore, He can't allow sin inside the kingdom of heaven. Since you were born with sin, you're a sinner. That means you'll never get to heaven as you are.

But you just said that God loves me so much He wants me to be in heaven with Him forever and ever and ever.

That's right. He does love you that much. And that's why He decided to make a way for you to get to heaven. Since the punishment for sin is death, God decided to send His Son Jesus to pay the death penalty for your sin so you wouldn't have to. You see, with Jesus paying the price for *you,* you can enter heaven on *His* behalf.

I'm starting to understand.

Imagine it like this: You're standing at the gates of heaven. It's a perfect and glorious kingdom with Almighty

and Holy God on the throne. You can't even stand before Him because of the sin in your life. So Jesus stands in front of you.

Between God and me?

Exactly. So now when God looks at you, He looks through His Son to see you. And when He looks through Jesus, He's looking through the One who never sinned.

Imagine this: God asks His Son, "Jesus, why should I let this young lady into My perfect kingdom?"

And from where He stands in front of you, Jesus says, "Because I have paid the death penalty for her sin. She's been forgiven by My holy blood. She is now spotless."

Know what God will say? I imagine Him stretching out His arms and saying, "Come here. I've been waiting and waiting for this moment to happen. I'm so glad you accepted My Son's sacrifice for your sins. Look! I've been preparing a special place for you to live. I built it myself. Come on. Let me show you around."

Wow.

Yeah! Double wow. What an incredible secret, huh?

I want that!

Okay, then the first step is prayer. That's how you establish a personal relationship with Jesus Christ and get to know God. Wanna do that right now?

Yes, already!

Okay. I'm going to pray a prayer, and I invite you to repeat this prayer after me:

> *Dear Jesus:*
>
> *I admit I'm a sinner. I understand I was born with sin. I've wanted my own way, and I've been selfish. I've taken charge of my life when I should have released control to You. But I am so sorry. I confess my sins. I repent of them now. I know that sin breaks*

3
23

Your heart, and I don't want to break Your heart any-more. Will You forgive me?

I believe the Bible is Your Holy Word, and I believe Your Holy Word is absolute Truth. I accept the Bible as Your divine inspiration that will help me know what to do in life and how to please You. I realize the Bible says if I ask Your forgiveness, You will forgive. And I believe You keep Your Word. So I accept Your forgiveness now, Jesus. Thank You so much!

I don't have the words to tell You how grateful I am that You died a terrible death on an ugly cross for my sins. You died so I wouldn't have to! Wow! I want to spend the rest of my days thanking You by the way I live my life.

So help me live in obedience to You. I love You, Jesus. I give You complete control of my life. It's not going to be "my way" any longer. I want Your way, Your will, and Your plan.

Thanks so much for letting me in on the holy secret that I can live forever and ever and ever with You in heaven. Teach me how to grow stronger in You. Amen.

+ + + + + + + + + + + + + + + + + +

Guess what! The Bible tells us that all of heaven rejoices when one of God's children comes to Him. That's you! Because you've given control of your life to God, and because you've accepted His precious gift of salvation, there's a party going on right now in the kingdom of heaven!

Ready to use your pen again? Paraphrase (put into your own words) this verse in the box provided. "I tell

you...there will be more rejoicing in heaven over one sinner who repents than over ninety-nine righteous persons who do not need to repent" (Luke 15:7 *NIV*).

_____'s Paraphrase of Luke 15:7
(write your name here)

_____

_____

_____

_____

_____

_____

_____

_____

_____

_____

_____

_____

_____

_____

_____

_____

_____

_____

_____

Here's what I'm thinking about after reading this chapter...

Discovering More
of the Secret

Major congrats! If you prayed that prayer, you're on your way to becoming a Secret Power Girl like Natasha and Emily.

You've just established the most important relationship in your life—a relationship with Jesus Christ, the Creator of the world!

And this is just the beginning!

Whaddya mean?

Flip back to page 22. Remember, we talked about establishing and maintaining a relationship with Jesus through a series of steps?

Oh, yeah!

And prayer was your first step. In fact, let's do a quick recap.

To become a Christian you gotta:

* realize that everyone has sinned (even you!).
  (Proof: Romans 3:23)

* realize the penalty for your sin is death.
  (Proof: Romans 6:23)

★ realize that Jesus Christ died for your sins.
(Proof: Romans 5:8)

★ realize that to be forgiven of your sin, you must
believe and confess that Jesus is Lord and that He
is the only way to receive salvation.
(Proof: Romans 10:8-10)

By praying that prayer in the last chapter, you demon-
strated to God that you understand the above "You
Gottas." But there is still a series of steps to be followed
to get the most out of your brand-new secret.

Consecration. This involves total surrender.
It's all about giving God your gifts and abilities
and desires to use for His glory.

I'm not sure I understand.

Let me introduce you to someone who's
already learned this part of the secret. I met Charity Allen
when she was 17 years old. She and her family were on
vacation in Colorado Springs, and Charity stopped at the
office where I work on *Brio* magazine. The vivacious
blond-haired, blue-eyed bundle of enthusiasm bounced
into my office and said, "Hi, I'm Charity. And I get *Brio*
magazine."

"Great to meet you, Charity. Sit down and tell me about
yourself."

"Okay. Well, I'll be a senior at the L.A. High School of
Performing Arts."

"Wow. That sounds pretty important. Do some of the students there get cast in commercials and TV shows?"

"Oh, yeah," she said. "Happens all the time."

"So tell me about someone who got cast in something.
Maybe I saw him on TV," I begged, always wanting to
hear a good story.

"Well, I was recently cast in NBC's *Another World*."

"Really?" I exclaimed.

"Yeah, but I turned it down."

"What happened?" I said.

Charity's Story

"Well...it started like this: I was sitting in Spanish class conjugating verbs, when my music teacher knocked on the door and asked to see me. When I walked into the hall, he was grinning from ear to ear.

'This is it, Charity,' he said. 'This is your big break!'

'What are you talking about?'

'I just got a call from a Hollywood casting agent for a lead soap opera. Apparently they've lost a lot of their younger viewers and want to do something to gain a younger audience. So they've decided to establish a brand-new female lead in *Another World*. They've already auditioned approximately 2,000 girls and haven't found the right one. So the casting agent just called me and asked if we have anyone at this school who fits the description of a young, blond bombshell who can sing and act. Charity, that's you! You fit the description!'

"Well, I told him my parents didn't even let me watch soap operas, and I didn't know if they'd let me audition for one!"

"So what happened?" I begged.

"I called home," Charity said. "Mom told me I could get the information and audition and we'd talk and pray about it as a family."

The casting agent faxed Charity's music teacher a script and the background of her character. Charity quickly memorized lines while her teacher drove her into Hollywood. After reading, some light blocking, and interviewing with the casting professional, Charity quietly sat down in the plush office.

The woman sat on the edge of her mahogany desk and looked Charity right in the eye. "Charity," she began, "you're exactly whom we're looking for. The part is yours!"

Charity's head began to swim as the woman told her everything they'd do for the young high school student. The long list included a move to New York for her and her entire family, a furnished condo, a limousine to pick her up and take her to the studio every day, a private tutor on the set to ensure she'd receive her high school degree…the list went on and on.

Charity's family lived in a two-bedroom mobile home. There were five kids in her family. Seven people were crowded inside a mobile home with only one bathroom! She couldn't help but smile as she dreamed about having her very own bedroom and bathroom.

Say What?!

Another question loomed large in her mind. "My mom is a stay-at-home mom," Charity stated. "My dad teaches school. So we don't have a lot of money. Even though you'd provide us with housing, I'm not sure we'd be able to make ends meet living in the Big Apple."

"Oh, Charity," the agent said. "You don't understand. What you'll make each week will probably meet the needs of your family."

"What would I make?" Charity innocently asked.

"You'll start out somewhere between $15,000 and $20,000 a week."

"Whoa! That would pretty much cover the needs of *my* family," Charity said in a daze. "As well as a few hundred others," she muttered under her breath.

But as the dreams swam in Charity's mind, something else stirred in her heart—the commitment she'd made to Jesus Christ. She knew He had gifted her with the ability to sing and act. And she had consecrated those gifts to God. She wanted to use her talent to bring glory to Christ. Could she help build God's kingdom using her gifts and talents this way?

She scooted her chair closer to the mahogany desk and looked the casting agent in the eyes. "You've been very kind in telling me everything you'll do for me," she

began. "But now I need to tell you what I *won't* do for you.

"I won't smoke. Or drink. Or cuss. Or take God's name in vain. Or pretend to be sexually involved with anyone on the show. You see, I've consecrated myself—all of me, including my gifts and talents—to God's glory. So anything I wouldn't do in real life, I won't pretend to do in front of a camera. Think that'll be a problem?"

The agent explained that the producers wanted Charity's character to be a role model for the younger generation and assured her there wouldn't be a problem.

"I'll have the executives here next week," she said. "You can sign the contract then."

Charity Stands Tall

Charity and her family prayed all week. She was determined not to compromise. When she met with the executives from the series, she was also met with praise and enthusiasm. The contract was sitting out on the mahogany desk right next to the pen Charity would use to sign it.

As she began to sign her name, though, she stopped suddenly and looked at the agent. "Remember all that stuff I told you I wouldn't do last week?" Charity asked.

"I remember."

"Nothing's changed, right?"

The agent shuffled her feet, shifted her weight, and glanced at Charity's mom. "There have been a few minor changes, but nothing to be concerned about."

"Like what?" Charity pressed.

"Well, your character will become sexually involved with a married man. You'll become pregnant. You'll have an abortion. You'll then become sexually involved with a rock star. You'll start using drugs—"

Charity put the pen down. "I can't be a part of *Another World*, " she said. "I won't do it."

And she walked out of the office.

Fast Forward

Now jump ahead a few months. Charity is sitting in my office, remember? "Charity," I said, "it's been a while since that happened. Be honest with me. Have you had any regrets about your decision?"

"Honestly? Yes. A few weeks ago I was in line at the supermarket and glanced at the rack next to me. There was a soap opera magazine on the shelf, and guess who was on the cover? My replacement! So while I stood in line, I opened the mag and began reading about her. She talked about the hunk she got to co-star with. And she mentioned a lot of her perks from being on the show. My heart sank. I thought, *What have I given up?*

"But as I read further, I noticed she talked about the steamy sex scenes she played out in front of the camera. And when I read that, I knew I'd made the right decision. This great wave of peace overcame me. Yes, I know there's a difference between acting and real life, but if I have to pretend something in front of a camera that doesn't glorify God, I'd be compromising. I won't do that. I've consecrated my gifts and abilities—my entire *life* to Him."

+ + + + + + + + + + + + + + + + + + +

Wow. What a fantastic example of someone who understands the secret of not only giving her life to Christ but also following Him every single day by giving Him 100 percent!

Yeah, that IS a cool story. I've given my life to Christ, but I haven't actually given Him specifics; I mean, not in the way you're talking about; not like this consecration thing. I haven't dedicated my gifts to Him.

You can. And I can help you do it.

That's what I want. But I'm not even sure what my gifts are!

That's okay. We can pray about that, too.

We already prayed, remember?

Yeah, but prayer isn't something you just do one time, or even once in a while. Prayer is an ongoing process. Unless you had to, you probably wouldn't go a few days without talking to your best friend, right?

No kidding. When we're not talking at school, we're on the phone. And when we're not on the phone, we're instant-messaging each other on the computer.

God wants you to talk with Him even more than that. He wants you to feel free to tell Him everything and ask Him anything. So let's pray, okay?

> *Dear Jesus:*
>
> *I don't even know what my gifts are yet. But I know this: I want to consecrate them to You. Whatever gifts, abilities, talents, and skills You're giving me, I wanna use them to bring glory to You.*
>
> *So, right now, I place my gifts in Your hands. Help me discover what they are, and help me to use them wisely. I want people to know that You're the Giver of my gifts and abilities. In Your name I pray this, Amen.*

How'd Charity know what her gifts were? And does everyone have special gifts? How do I find out what mine are? Now that I've dedicated them to God, I'm anxious to find out what they are!

Great questions. Maybe it's time to get a refill on your drink and stock up on some more munchies. We'll get to all the stuff about gifts, but there's a pathway we need to follow. And guess what! That involves steps.

Oh, yeah! We're back to that series of steps you said I gotta follow.

Right. And if you're ready, we'll keep hiking.

Let's go!

Growing Strong
in the Secret

Now that you know you're a Christian, you realize you've tapped into a wonderful secret:

The fact that Jesus Christ will forgive your sins, give you eternal life, and equip you with the power you need for living a strong and holy life. Whew! That's a lot to swallow. And although this is a fantastic beginning, it's just that—the beginning!

In order to grow strong in Christ, you need to keep following the stepping stones. Ready for the next one?

 Read the Bible. If you don't have a Bible that's written in a way you can understand—get one! There are so many exciting student Bibles on the market now. Make a trip to your local Christian bookstore and find one with lots of explanatory notes—to help you understand what you're reading—and lots of graphics to keep your attention hooked on what you're reading.

Why is reading the Bible so important?

It's important because it's actually God speaking to us and because it helps you understand more about the secrets of God. And here's the cool thing: As you get to know Him better, you become more like Him.

Wow. That IS cool!

Check this out: "The whole Bible was given to us by inspiration from God and is useful to teach us what is true and to make us realize what is wrong in our lives; it

straightens us out and helps us do what is right. It is God's way of making us well prepared at every point, fully equipped to do good to everyone" (2 Timothy 3:16-17 *The Living Bible*).

Time to grab your pen. Let's take a quick quiz about the above verse.

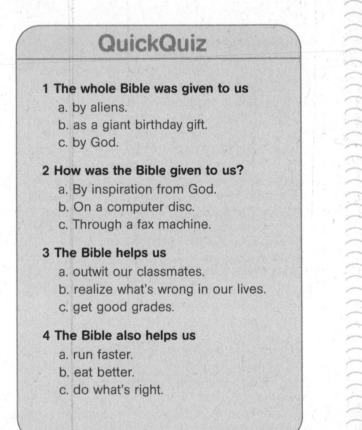

QuickQuiz

1 The whole Bible was given to us
   a. by aliens.
   b. as a giant birthday gift.
   c. by God.

2 How was the Bible given to us?
   a. By inspiration from God.
   b. On a computer disc.
   c. Through a fax machine.

3 The Bible helps us
   a. outwit our classmates.
   b. realize what's wrong in our lives.
   c. get good grades.

4 The Bible also helps us
   a. run faster.
   b. eat better.
   c. do what's right.

It's just a fact. If you want to become strong in the secret power and wisdom of Christ, you need to read the Bible. Think of it as His personal letter to you.

When should I read it?

Try to read it every single day. It doesn't matter if you read it in the morning, afternoon, or at night—just read it. Even if you only read for one minute a day, you'll be surprised at the incredible difference it will make in your life.

Try to make your Bible reading a good habit—you know—like brushing your teeth. You know how you don't always LIKE to brush your teeth but you always do? You do it because it's the right thing to do. (And because if you don't, your teeth will eventually fall out. Then when you try to say, "Hi, my name's Haylie," it'll sound like, "I, yi yay's Yaylie," and people will look at you funny because you sound like a foreigner but look like a local and when all your friends are eating corn-on-the-cob, you'll take a piece too, because you wanna be included and be like everyone else, only you won't be able to get any of the corn off because you have no teeth, but you'll try anyway because you don't want anyone to find out you're different, and you'll try to lip it off or scrape a few kernels with your gums but it just won't work and eventually the people sitting around you WILL notice and they'll put down their own ears of corn to stare at you and 30 minutes later, when your gums are bleeding and you've still got a full ear of corn on your cob, you'll realize your friends are all laughing and pointing and saying, "Hey, what's with Yaylie? She's, like, our age but she like has no teeth and it's totally gross like in a major way." And finally they'll all get up to leave because their corn is cold and they don't want it anymore, and you'll be left alone with bleeding gums and butter smeared all over your face, with some salt and pepper dabbed on for good measure, and you'll WISH you had just brushed your teeth when your parents TOLD you to, instead of only wetting the toothbrush and squeezing some toothpaste by the sink drain to fool them. See, you can fool them part of the time, but eventually it's YOU who'll end up with no teeth, no friends—but with greasy Parkay all over your skin—sitting all alone writing run-on sentences.)

Well, reading the Bible is kind of like that. You just need to develop it as a good habit, because if you don't, you'll

eventually end up a mess.

Take a quick peek at Colossians 2:7 and copy it down in the space provided.

Go to church. Being involved with the Body of Christ (other Christians) on a regular basis helps you grow. It's important to worship God and learn from a spiritual leader—a pastor, priest, or evangelist. Hopefully, the church you attend has a youth group. It's exciting to study the Bible and learn about God with other students your age. But even if your church doesn't have a youth group, you can

still grow strong in Christ by plugging into your church and finding a ministry.

Whaddya mean—finding a ministry?

Participating in a ministry means getting involved in something that helps other people and brings glory to God. It means spending time meeting others' needs.

Yeah, yeah, yeah—I know you're busy. But God's had it with some of our ridiculous excuses:

* I had to bleach my jeans so I could get that coveted faded look. (Oops, it's never right to covet. In fact, it's one of the Ten Commandments. Grab your Bible and flip over to Exodus 20:17 and copy it down in the space provided.)

_____

_____

_____

_____

_____

_____

* My accordion was out of tune. (What does that have to do with anything?)

* It's my night to clean the kitchen. (How hard is it to throw McDonald's wrappers in the trash?)

* My cat is in labor. (Unless you're a trained veterinarian, this excuse isn't going to fly either.)

* I would go to youth group tonight, but I just have too much homework. And if I don't do my home-work, I'll be tempted to cheat. (No way. Don't even go there. Did you know cheating is the same as stealing? When you cheat, you're taking something that doesn't belong to you. And stealing is breaking another one of the Ten Commandments. When you get used to stealing answers that aren't yours, what's going to happen when you get used to tak-ing other things that aren't yours? Like, you know, that bottle of body butter from Bath & Body Works or that grand piano you've had your eye on or the scuba equipment you've always wanted or those fake toenails for your feet? And when you start tak-ing stuff like that, it's only a matter of time before you get caught. And when you get caught, you could end up in jail with a bunch of hardened crim-inals who have stolen stuff like cereal and athletic socks and Nike shoes, and you'll be scared to death of having to share a prison cell with one of them because if they've stolen cereal, who knows? They may wanna steal your teeth. And you'll be afraid to sleep at night because you think you might snore and when you snore your mouth falls open and your cellmate will be tempted to stick a pair of pliers inside your open mouth and steal some of your teeth. See what cheating can get you? Just don't go there. Ever!)

So make it a point not only to attend church but to get involved as well. Find a ministry that fits your interests and abilities. Let's make a list of ministry ideas, okay? I'll get you started, and you finish it. Use your imagination!

* Help out in the nursery.

* Volunteer to rake and pick up leaves from the church lawn.

* Join the choir.

Growing Stronger
in the Secret

According to what you learned in the last chapter, growing strong in the secret of Christ means:

(circle all that apply)

    a. developing a ministry.

    b. getting a new hobby.

    c. adopting a pet from the animal shelter.

    d. going to church.

    e. rearranging your closet.

    f. brushing your teeth.

    g. reading your Bible.

Let's keep following the series of steps on this exciting hike toward drawing closer to Christ, okay?

STEP 5

Develop a strong prayer life. Prayer is simply talking to God...and listening. Every single Secret Power Girl in the world has a strong prayer life. And what could be more exciting than getting to talk on a first-name basis with the King of Kings?

But I never know what to say to God.

Tell Him everything. Are you worried about passing the history test? Tell Him. Excited about Friday night's football game? Let Him know. Don't like the school cafeteria food? He wants to know about it. Concerned about your parents? Pray for them.

There's nothing too big or too small to pray about.

REPEAT: There's nothing too big or too small to pray about.

Okay, say it out loud now: There's *nothing* too big or too small to pray about.

It's a fact: God cares about every single detail in your life. He even knows how many hairs are on your head! Need proof? Take a look at Matthew 10:30-31 in your Bible and copy the verses in the box below.

The Bible tells us to pray about everything. Check this out: "Do not be anxious about anything, but in every-thing, by prayer and petition, with thanksgiving, present your requests to God. And the peace of God, which transcends all understanding, will guard your hearts and your minds in Christ Jesus" (Philippians 4:6-7 *NIV*).

Grab your pen! It's time for another quick quiz.

QuickQuiz

1 According to the above verse, what should we pray about?

_____

2 If you're worried or anxious about something, what's the solution?

_____

3 What do we receive from God when we give Him our prayer requests?

_____

4 What kind of peace does God give?

_____

5 If you need peace in your life, how can you get it?

_____

6 What does God promise to guard your heart and mind with if you'll pray?

_____

A Very Special Prayer

Jesus thought talking to His heavenly Father was so important, He did it every day. If *Jesus* needed to pray every day, how much more we need to do it! Prayer was so important to Him, He also made a point of teaching His disciples how to pray. We call this specific prayer the "Lord's Prayer." It shows us what to pray for and how to address our heavenly Father.

Before reading any further, grab your Bible and read the Lord's Prayer in Matthew 6:9-13. After you've read it, you can sign your name, pass GO, and move on. (But not until after you've read it!)

I READ THE

LORD'S PRAYER

_____

SIGNATURE

 GO! Keep moving. Carry on. Straight ahead. Get going!

One More Thing About Prayer

Have you ever thought about the power that's available to you through prayer? Think about it: All of God's power—which he used to create the entire universe—is available to you through this line of communication we call prayer. God *wants* to hear you pray. He desires to

meet your needs.

Meet Juanita. She's 75, but many years ago when her two children were small, Juanita was broke. Her husband had died, and she did the best she could to provide for her 3-year-old daughter and her 5-year-old son. She took every odd job she could find, but there just wasn't much work in her Mexican village. One month, the money simply ran out.

Juanita was a Secret Power Girl. She had established a personal, growing relationship with Jesus Christ, and she knew the power of prayer. So she gave her request to God. In fact, she prayed for three hours about what to do.

She sensed God was directing her to a large market called El Dorado in a nearby village. So she obeyed and went to the market. It was huge! There were more than 100 checkout lanes. She was overwhelmed. But she kept praying as she entered the market and sensed God leading her to fill a grocery cart with enough groceries to last her family for three months.

Confused, but wanting to be obedient, she wheeled the cart through the various aisles and filled it with three months' necessities. As she approached the checkout counters, she sensed God leading her to checkout lane number seven. There was only one customer in line.

Juanita rolled her cart behind the gentleman in front of her, but when the cashier finished bagging the man's groceries, she placed a CLOSED sign on the conveyor belt and said, "Sorry, I'm closed. It's time for my lunch break. You'll need to go to another line."

Juanita stood behind her cart, looked the cashier in the eyes, and politely said, "No, my Father told me to come here. I'll wait."

The cashier shrugged her shoulders, and Juanita stood patiently beside her cart for 45 minutes. The cashier eventually returned, removed the sign, and turned on her cash register. Juanita began to unload her groceries onto the conveyor belt and watched as the cashier rang them up one at a time.

When the next-to-the-last item was being rung up, the manager's voice interrupted the noise of the market.

"Attention, Shoppers! Today is the seventh-year anniversary of El Dorado Market. We're celebrating by giving everything free to whomever is being checked out at this moment in lane seven!"

+ + + + + + + + + + + + + + + + + +

My first reaction to this story was "YES, YES, YES!" But as I thought about it, I realized that's exactly the kind of ending I *should* have expected. After all, doesn't God promise to meet all of our needs? (Read what Jesus says about how God takes care of us in Luke 12:22-31)

There's a verse in the Old Testament that reminds us just how intently He's watching our lives: "For the eyes of the Lord search back and forth across the whole earth, looking for people whose hearts are perfect toward him, so that he can show his great power in helping them" (2 Chronicles 16:9 *The Living Bible*).

Those eyes do not belong to a "traffic cop God" who's just waiting to write us up for something we've done wrong. Those are the eyes of a loving, giving Father who's looking for an opportunity to jump into *your* life during *your* day and lift your load. He wants to make your day a better one! But you'll never know how much He has to offer unless you spend time talking with Him every single day.

So develop a strong prayer life. Everything in your life will make more sense if you do. You see, God wants to be your best friend, but He also wants to be

your **Savior,**

your **Guide,**

your **Counselor,**

your Redeemer,

your Physician,

your Shelter,

your God.

So let Him be all He wants to be in your life. And how do you do that? By developing a strong prayer life. Do it—and be amazed at the difference it will make!

Here's what I'm thinking about after reading this chapter...

Understanding the Truth

Do you need a refill on your drink? Still got some munchies on hand?

If not, this is a great time to grab some brain food because we're getting into an exciting part of the journey! So go ahead. I'll wait right here. (If you already have your munchies, we'll just sit here a second and wait for everyone else, okay? And while we're waiting, let's make a list of some of our fave munchies, okay? I'll leave some space so you'll have room to include yours.)

carrots	sunflower seeds
Cracker Jacks	milk
lemonade	apples
broccoli	_____
cereal	_____
cauliflower	_____
graham crackers	_____
celery sticks	_____

STEP 7

Access the power of the Holy Spirit. Without the Holy Spirit reigning in your life, it's only a matter of time before you run out of steam. You've probably heard about the Holy Spirit, but do you understand who and what He is?

Not really. I've heard about the Father, the Son, and the Holy Spirit. But I don't really get it. But hey! We went from step five to Step 7. You skipped a step!

Wow. Can't slip anything past you! Way to pay attention. I did it on purpose. Tee-hee!

How come?

Because I want you to know what Step 7 is and then we're gonna back up to step six.

So I'm kind of looking into the future and then backing up.

Yes! You know how sometimes you want to know what's going to happen later on in the book, so you flip forward a few pages then come back to where you were?

How'd you know I do that?

Because I do it, too. Only this book saves you the trouble. Instead of having to flip forward, I'm just telling you—then we'll hike back to where we were.

Cool. Okay. Keep going.

All right. Think about this: The Father is God. The Son is Jesus. And the Holy Spirit is our Counselor, Comfortor, and Teacher who guides us to the truth. This might be a little tough to swallow, but here goes: All three are really one—yet even though they're one, they're still three.

Okay, I admit I've never been good at math. So you pretty much lost me right there.

Again, it *is* tough to understand; and we won't *fully* understand it all until we get to heaven. (Okay, here's where we're taking a step back. In honor of this backward step, stand up and walk backward while counting from 10 to one. Then sit back down, and we'll be back at Step 6, okay?)

 Know what really happened. But God has always existed. "In the beginning was the Word, and the Word was with God, and the Word was God. He was with God in the beginning" (John 1:1-2 *NIV*).

The *Word* is Christ and represents the wisdom and power

of God and the first cause of all things—God's personal expression of Himself to men. Christ is part of God, and He's also one with God. To make Himself known to mankind, God separated the Christ part of Himself and sent Him to earth in the form of a human being.

And that's where the Christmas story begins!

Exactly. Jesus Christ was born of the Virgin Mary. He grew as a boy and became a man. "And Jesus grew in wisdom and stature, and in favor with God and men" (Luke 2:52 *NIV*).

When Jesus was 30 years old, He began His public ministry by proclaiming how God wanted to forgive men of their sins and offer them eternal life. The religious leaders got really mad and thought, *Who does this man think he is—telling us what God thinks and wants?*

So Jesus told them straight out that He was able to say these things because He and the Father were actually one! "Anyone who has seen me has seen the Father. Don't you believe that I am in the Father, and that the Father is in me? The words I say to you are not just my own. Rather, it is the Father, living in me, who is doing his work. Believe me when I say that I am in the Father and the Father is in me" (John 14:9-11 *NIV*).

The religious leaders became angrier and refused to believe Jesus—even though He did several miracles that proved He and God were one. The religious leaders (Pharisees, scribes, Sadducees) called this blasphemy and after failing to trap Him several times, they finally struck a deal with Judas—one of Christ's disciples—to hand the Lord over to a mob of angry people who hauled Him into court.

Yeah, and I can't believe that Judas wigged out and betrayed Jesus! What a loser he must have been.

Well, Judas wasn't a loser when Christ chose him as a disciple. Jesus prayed all night about the 12 He would choose to mentor and train as disciples. Judas had to have some great qualities for him to be selected to be part of such a group. He was a Zealot—a member of a

political group that wanted to overthrow Rome and give the Jews more rights, status, and freedom. And that wasn't a bad goal. The Jews were mistreated by the Romans and taxed too heavily. Judas was also good with numbers because the other 11 disciples elected him to be treasurer of the group.

But somewhere along the way, Judas must have stopped listening to Jesus' sermons. He must have turned a deaf ear to His love and a blind eye to His miracles. Perhaps some bitterness began to fester. After all, many of the 12 disciples were from a specific part of the country. Judas wasn't. He didn't have their accent. He didn't have relatives in the group. He had no childhood friends among the 12. Peter and Andrew were brothers. John and James were brothers. And Peter, Andrew, John, and James all worked in the fishing business together. They had family ties and childhood secrets. They were a tight-knit foursome.

Phillip and Nathaniel were also friends when they became disciples. And it wasn't that the 11 disciples excluded Judas—again, they gave him their vote of admiration and trust by putting him in charge of the group's finances. But it could be that Judas just never felt part of the group. If so, it was his own fault.

I don't think he woke up one morning and simply said, "I'm gonna betray Jesus." There are always backward steps taken when one walks away from the Lord. The disciples later found out that Judas had been dipping into the treasury for his own personal means. Maybe he never committed his selfishness to God. Perhaps he hadn't surrendered his rights to the Lord.

Many Bible scholars believe Judas didn't really understand he was betraying Jesus unto death; that he didn't realize—until it was too late—that the mob would actually kill Christ.

Many scholars believe Judas betrayed Jesus into the hands of the authorities because he thought it would "make" Jesus hurry and set up His kingdom. Christ had often told His disciples that He was establishing a new

Kingdom—the Kingdom of God. They thought He was talking about an earthly kingdom. *Great!* they thought. *He's going to overthrow the Roman government and set up a new kingdom. He'll be in charge, of course, but we'll be right there on the front lines with Him in places of importance.*

Christ knew they didn't get it. And He continued to tell them His Kingdom was not of this earth. Over and over again He commanded them to love their Roman neighbors—not overtake them.

Judas grew impatient. He wanted the Romans out of control and thought Jesus was just the One to take charge. He'd seen the miracles. He knew of Christ's power. And he wanted to be a part of this zealous and exciting political takeover. So Judas turned Jesus over to the authorities thinking, *Now we'll show Rome! Finally, we'll be in charge!*

The problem? Jesus never planned a political takeover. And no one puts the Lord of all creation on a human timetable. Jesus will act in His holy timing—not ours!

Wow. I never knew all that. It sure makes the whole story more interesting to know those details.

If you're going to be sure about what you believe, you need to *understand* what you believe!

I think I understand it much better now! Keep going, okay?

What Christ endured during the next several hours was horrendous and illegal.

Illegal?

Yes. Even before His trial began, it had already been determined that Jesus must die.

That's not fair!

No, it's not. It's illegal. Let's look at what the Bible says. In this verse Caiaphas, the high priest, is speaking: " 'You do not realize that it is better for you that one man die for the people than that the whole nation perish.' He prophesized that Jesus would die...so from that day on they plotted to take [Jesus'] life" (John 11:50, 53 *NIV*).

And check this out: "Now the Passover and the Feast of Unleavened Bread were only two days away, and the chief priests and the teachers of the law were looking for some sly way to arrest Jesus and kill him" (Mark 14:1 *NIV*).

I never realized that!

That's not the only illegal thing that happened. False witnesses were bribed to make up lies about Jesus and testify against Him.

But that's not right! They can't do that!

Again, it was illegal. Let's look at the Scripture: "The chief priests and the whole Sanhedrin were looking for false evidence against Jesus so that they could put him to death. But they did not find any, though many false witnesses came forward" (Matthew 26:59 *NIV*).

That really ticks me off!

More illegal stuff:

* No defense for Jesus was sought or allowed.

* The High Priest put Jesus under oath, but then incriminated Him for what He said. (Matthew 26:63-66)

* Cases involving such serious crimes were to be tried only in the Sanhedrin's regular meeting place, not in the High Priest's courtyard!

* After Jesus was led to Pilate, the charges against Him were changed.

You can't do that in a court of law—can you?

No. Totally illegal.

Okay. So let's pretend I'm a lawyer and I'm prosecuting someone for stealing a laptop computer. So the trial is going along and all of a sudden I say, "No, I got confused. It really wasn't a laptop he stole—it was a car!" The judge would think I was crazy!

Exactly. But that's what happened with Jesus. He was initially charged with blasphemy based on His statement that He could destroy and rebuild the Temple of God in three days.

Yeah, I'm not sure I get that.

Everyone thought He was talking about a physical building—the temple. But He was referring to Himself as the Temple of God; He would be destroyed (crucified) and conquer death three days later.

Okay, I get it now.

But when He was brought before Pilate, the charges against Him were changed to Jesus' claim to be a king and His disagreement with paying taxes to the Romans.

Hey! I think I remember a Bible story about Jesus and a coin and the taxes and stuff. Does that fit here?

Exactly! Jesus never told people not to pay their taxes. In fact, He encouraged them to pay the government what they owed. Let's look at what really happened:

> [The Pharisees said], "Tell us then, what is your opinion? Is it right to pay taxes to Caesar or not?"
>
> But Jesus, knowing their evil intent, said, "You hypocrites, why are you trying to trap me? Show me the coin used for paying the tax." They brought him a denarius, and he asked them, "Whose portrait is this? And whose inscription?"
>
> "Caesar's," they replied.
>
> Then he said to them, "Give to Caesar what is Caesar's, and to God what is God's." (Matthew 22:17-21 *NIV*)

So His accusers lied again.

Correct. And you know the rest of the story: Jesus was crucified on an ugly, splintered, wooden cross. He died for the sins of the world. And do you know what's so cool about that?

What?

He didn't have to do it. He could have called an army of angels from heaven to kill all His accusers. He could have commanded nature to rise up and establish an earthquake, a tornado, or a giant fire. He could have done any number of things. But He chose to remain on the cross out of love.

Because He loved the people who hung Him there?

Yes—but not only them. He also did it because He loved you.

I wasn't there! I wasn't even born yet.

But Jesus knew you even before you were born. The Bible tells us He knew you even before you were being formed inside your mom's womb. "You made all the delicate, inner parts of my body, and knit them together in my mother's womb. Thank you for making me so wonderfully complex! It is amazing to think about. Your workmanship is marvelous—and how well I know it. You were there while I was being formed in utter seclusion! You saw me before I was born and scheduled each day of my life before I began to breathe. Every day was recorded in your Book!" (Psalm 139:13-16 *The Living Bible*).

Whoa! That's amazing. I never thought of it that way before.

Believe it! While Jesus Christ was hanging on the cross, He was thinking about *you*—even though you hadn't been born yet. And He chose to stay on the cross and die an excruciating, horrible death so you wouldn't have to. He wanted to pay the price for your sins.

Wow. That gives His death a whole new meaning.

It gives it a very personal meaning, doesn't it?

Sure does.

And you probably know what happened next. Jesus died and was buried. But three days later, He conquered death and rose from the grave.

That's Easter!

Exactly. We celebrate His resurrection (rising from the dead) and rejoice because we serve a LIVING Savior.

I have friends who are Muslim, Buddhists, and other religions. Do they know about Jesus conquering death?

They may—and they may not. That's why it's important for you to let them in on this incredible secret! And when you think about it, Jesus' resurrection is what separates us from all other religions.

Whaddya mean?

The other religious leaders died, were buried, and their remains are still resting in the grave. Christ's grave is empty. He's the real thing. The others were false teachers. They were just human. They lived and they died. But God Almighty lived in human form (as Jesus Christ), died, rose from the dead, and still lives—right now!

In heaven.

Right. And that's what brings us to the next exciting step in our journey.

What?

Sorry. You're gonna have to wait till the next chapter. I need a refill on my Coke. Take a quick break and meet me on the next page in five minutes, okay?

You got it!

Plug Into the Power
(Part One)

8

Before we hike forward, it's time to use your gel pen. Ready for a quick quiz? Here we go!

QuickQuiz

1 God is:
a. the Father
b. a rainbow,
c. all plant life

2 Jesus is:
a. the speed of light
b. the Son
c. a prophet

3 The Holy Spirit is:
a. New Age stuff
b. a different religion
c. the strength and presence of God and Christ

4 God came to earth
a. and left quickly.
b. in the form of a man named Jesus.
c. to destroy it.

5 Jesus was born (circle all correct answers)
a. in a manger

b. at a Holiday Inn in Bethlehem.

c. of the Virgin Mary.

d. to start a new political group.

e. so we could learn of God's forgiveness of our sins through Christ.

6 Which disciple betrayed Jesus to the authorities?

a. Nathaniel

b. Andrew

c. Judas

d. James

7 The trials of Jesus were

a. held in a fancy courtroom.

b. illegal, held at night, and with false witnesses.

c. completely fair with reliable witnesses.

8 Jesus died because

a. He was too scared to fight back.

b. He wanted to frighten the disciples.

c. He wanted to pay the penalty of sin for mankind.

9 Jesus' death proves

a. His amazing love for us.

b. Judas was really smart to betray Him.

c. His lawyers gave up.

10 Resurrection is a fancy word that means

a. Jesus grew in stature and wisdom.

b. Jesus did many miracles while on earth.

c. Jesus rose from the dead.

11 After Jesus ascended (went up to heaven),

a. His disciples disbanded and gave up.

b. everyone had to go to school.

c. He left the Holy Spirit in His place.

d. We haven't covered this yet.

Okay, that last question is sort of a trick question. The correct answer is C, but D is also correct—that's what this chapter is all about.

The God and Christ stuff makes sense now. But where does the Holy Spirit come in?

Glad you asked! Let's eavesdrop on a conversation Jesus had with His disciples before He ascended back to heaven, okay?

Are you sure it's okay to eavesdrop?

Sure! In fact, Jesus WANTS you to eavesdrop on ALL of His conversations. That's why He included them in the Bible.

Oh, I get it.

The Characters: *Jesus and 11 disciples.* (Judas had already left the room to find the authorities.)

The Scene: *The Last Supper. They have just finished communion. They broke the bread, which Christ said symbolized His body, and they drank the juice, which Christ announced was the symbol of His blood.*

The Plot: *Jesus is explaining to the remaining disciples what will happen next. They are confused, shocked, and full of questions.*

The Conversation: *Jesus is speaking*: " 'If you love me, you will obey what I command. And I will ask the Father, and he will give you another Counselor to be with you forever—the Spirit of truth' " (John 14:15-17 *NIV*).

Since Jesus was getting ready to physically leave the earth, He wanted His disciples to know that He wouldn't leave them hanging. He would leave them with His very Spirit. And that's what we call the Holy Spirit.

As Jesus said, the Holy Spirit acts as a counselor—He helps us know what to do. He's also the embodiment of Truth. Have you ever felt "checked" about something?

Yeah. Like when I started to sneak outta the house one night to go my friend's house, but I don't know…I couldn't do it. Something felt weird. I knew it was wrong.

That was the Holy Spirit. Once a person has accepted Jesus Christ as their Lord and Savior, the Holy Spirit is allowed to work through a person's conscience, heart, and mind.

Wow. The Holy Spirit was talking to me when I was trying to sneak out?

Yes. He acts as absolute Truth in our lives. He "checks" us about the wrong things and guides us in the right direction.

Sort of like a built-in compass?

Yes. But you have a responsibility, too.

What's that?

That's the next step in our journey.

STEP 7

Access the power of the Holy Spirit. The Holy Spirit is Truth, but He's also POWER! Remember the mighty miracles Christ did while He was on earth?

Yeah. He made blind men see and He healed deaf people. And He even raised Lazarus from the dead!

Yes, and that's a lot of power! When Jesus left the earth physically to return to heaven, He said He'd send His Spirit to guide us, help us, comfort us, and empower us. So without the Holy Spirit reigning in our lives, we're running on empty.

I don't get it.

The Holy Spirit is our power source. He's plugged into God who is all-powerful and all-knowing. When we're plugged into the Holy Spirit, we're also plugged into God and all His mighty power.

Whoa!

Double whoa! Triple whoa! Think of the Holy Spirit as sort of an electrical socket.

Okay.

And think of yourself as the electrical cord.

I'm an electrical cord?

Work with me. It's an example.

Okay. I'm an electrical cord.

The cord by itself doesn't hold any power, does it?

No. But I have wires inside me.

Right. You do. You're fully wired, but unless you plug into the electrical outlet, you don't have any power coursing through your wires. See, that electrical outlet represents the Holy Spirit. Your wires represent your relationship to Jesus Christ. You may be fully wired—you pray every now and then and even read your Bible once in a while—but that's an incomplete life. What good is a wired cord with no power? When you plug the cord into the electrical outlet, however, you get all kinds of power running through you.

High voltage!

Exactly! And as long as you remain plugged into the power source, you'll operate with power.

Hmmm. I'm starting to get it. But I need a little more. Keep going.

In order for you to live the holy life God desires for you, you need a supernatural power. Admit it, you're only human. How in the world can you live a holy life in your own power?

I can't! I'd need something outta this world to accomplish that!

And that's exactly where the Holy Spirit comes into play. See, the God you serve isn't a God of frustration. No way would He say, "Live a holy life. Good luck. You probably won't make it. But that's My command anyway."

Your God says, "Live a holy life—and here's how to do it: I'll equip you with everything you need to make that possible. I'll give you My supernatural power—My Holy Spirit. And *in My Spirit's power,* I'll enable you to live a godly life."

Wow.

Check this out: "Be holy, because I am holy" (Leviticus 11:44 *NIV*) and "But just as he who called you is holy, so be holy in all you do; for it is written, 'Be holy, because I am holy' " (1 Peter 1:15-16 *NIV*).

It's absolutely impossible for any of us to be holy without the Holy Spirit's power reigning in our lives.

Well, how do I get that power?

Ahha! Pay close attention, okay?

Yeah, yeah, yeah.

Remember way back at the beginning of this book when we talked about Emily and Natasha who had some kind of secret?

> Power: The ability to act or do. Possession of control, authority, or influence over others. Authority. Might. A force or energy that is or can be applied to work.

Yes. And I found out their secret is a strong relationship with Jesus Christ.

We also briefly chatted about how it seemed as though they had some kind of special power, remember?

Oh, yeah! They were both so confident. And so was Charity Allen—the girl who turned down the part in the soap opera and all that money!

This is the next part of their secret: They DO have a special power! They have the power of the Holy Spirit. They've learned the secret of accessing His supernatural power!

How do I get the Holy Spirit?

Well, in a sense, you already have Him.

I do?

Yes. When you committed your life to Jesus Christ, you accepted Him into your heart. You told Him that you wanted to live for Him. When Jesus came into your life, *all* of Him came in. You didn't get just a little bit of Jesus. You got God (the Father), Jesus (the Son), and the Holy Spirit (the power of God and Jesus).

Then how come I don't live with any kind of power?

Because you haven't accessed it yet. Think back to the

electrical cord. It's wired. The power is ready to course through the cord and light up an entire room. But that power has to be accessed. It's there. It's just not being used at the moment.

So how do I get it and use it and live with it?

Ahhh. Great question. And again—that's part of the secret. The power—and accessing it—is an exciting part of this whole secret in Christ.

Here's what I'm thinking about after reading this chapter...

_____

_____

_____

_____

_____

_____

_____

_____

_____

_____

_____

_____

_____

_____

_____

_____

_____

Plug Into the Power
(Part Two)

Let's put your gel pen to use, okay?

Before we continue hiking on our secret power journey, let's get some stuff down about the Holy Spirit.

Look up this verse in your Bible and copy it here in the space provided: John 6:63.

According to John 15:26, where does the Holy Spirit get His truth?

After John the Baptist baptized Jesus, the Holy Spirit (in the form of a dove) came upon Him. Christ then went into the desert. Let's take a peek: "Jesus, full of the Holy Spirit, returned from the Jordan and was led by the Spirit in the desert, where for forty days he was tempted by the devil" (Luke 4:1-2 *NIV*).

If you'll continue reading the rest of that chapter, you'll discover Jesus was able to fight temptation because of the Holy Spirit ruling in His life.

Everyone is tempted. When you're tempted, what kind of difference could the Holy Spirit make in your life?

Read Matthew 12:28-29 and answer this question: What did the Holy Spirit's power enable Jesus to do?

Read Romans 8:16-17. Who bears witness to the fact that you are a child of God?

Now that you understand more about the Holy Spirit and His special power, let's continue our hike, okay?

Access the power of the Holy Spirit. We're still on Step 7. As we talked earlier, when you ask Jesus to invade your life, you get all of Him. But in order for you to truly live in the supernatural power of the Holy Spirit—He has to have all of YOU!

But I've already given my life to Christ, remember? And I've already consecrated my gifts to Him—even though I don't know what they are yet. What more can I do?

You can give Him your "unknown bundle."

What's that?

It's part of total surrender. There's a fancy word for it: *Sanctification.* What it really means is making Jesus LORD of your life. Living in radical obedience to His Lordship and in His power.

That's how Charity Allen was able to walk away from riches and fame. She was living in radical obedience to the Lordship of Christ. Even before she knew she would be offered that prestigious spot on a glamorous show, she had already given it to God.

But how could she have? She didn't even know about it yet! How can I give God what I don't know about?

That's what the unknown bundle is all about. It's coming to Christ in total surrender—

But I already came to Christ.

Right. And you don't have to start all over. It's not like, "Okay, I'll become a Christian for the fourteenth time now, and maybe this time it'll click." You're already a Christian. You've repented of your sins and have tapped into the secret of establishing and maintaining a strong, intimate growing relationship with Him.

Yeah.

So pray right here. Right at this point. Right where you are now. And in this prayer, you can give God your past, your present, and your future. Even though you don't know what your future holds—you can still place it in His hands.

I get it! The future is the unknown bundle!

Exactly. For instance, you don't know who you'll marry yet, but you can go ahead and give your future marriage to Christ.

Yeah! And I don't know who my kids will be someday—or even if they'll be boys or girls—but I can give them to God ahead of time . . . right now!

Yes! And here's the cool thing about what happens when you do that. When you give God EVERYTHING—including the unknown bundle—and give Him all of you, He releases the power of His Spirit (that's already residing in your wires) and saturates you with His supernatural power.

Wow!

Double wow. Triple wow! And in that power—you can live a holy life. Not in your own strength, but in His mighty power surging within you.

I want that!

See, God not only wants to be your best Friend, your Savior, and your Guide, He also wants to be your power supply, your energizer, and your strength to live *in* the world without being part *of* the world.

I need that!

THAT is the secret power!

Now. I want it right now!

Okay. Let's pray. As always, when we need something, we go to our heavenly Father. He's the One who's committed to supplying our needs. I'll pray, and you repeat the prayer after me, okay?

Okay.

> *Dear Jesus:*
>
> *Thanks that I'm already a Christian. Thanks that You've already forgiven my sins and have come into my life. I'm excited that I have been given eternal life as a gift from You.*
>
> *I realize that I have all of You…but You don't really have all of me yet. I want to change that right now. Jesus, I've already given You my heart and my sins and my gifts and talents. But now I want to give You my will. My self. My rights. My desires. My dreams. My plans. My goals.*
>
> *I give You my past and my present and my future. Jesus, I'm pretending I'm holding a box that's titled "unknown bundle" in my hands. I have no idea what's inside…but You know. I don't have a clue what it contains, but I'm giving it to You right now. All the stuff that's going to happen in my future now belongs to You.*
>
> *I give You my friends, my relationships, the guys I'll date, the man I'll marry, the children I'll have. I give You my career, my home, my wardrobe. I give it all, Jesus.*
>
> *I don't know what I'll face two weeks from now, but that battle is already Yours. I don't know who's going to hurt me in six months or what so-and-so will say about me behind my back tomorrow, but it belongs to You.*
>
> *So, Jesus, when those things happen and I start to get mad, please use Your Holy Spirit to remind me: "Wait a second. You don't have to fight with that. You already gave it to God, remember? It's His. Leave it in His control."*
>
> *I want to be saturated with Your supernatural*

power, Jesus. Will You cleanse me inside? Give me a spiritual bubble bath with Your Holy Spirit. Release the power of Your Holy Spirit within me right now. And help me to actually live in that power!

Thank You, Jesus! I realize—in this power—I can say no to temptation. I can turn the other cheek when I'm wronged. I can even die for You. I give You my rights. I don't own my life anymore. I'm totally Yours, Jesus.

Thank You for Your power that makes this commitment possible. In Your Name I pray these things. Amen.

Okay, now think about this: The same mighty power that raised Christ from the dead—the same mighty power that put the stars in the sky and set the whole world in motion—is YOURS to use and live in! That's a lot of power, huh?

High voltage!

Now you don't want that power to just sit inside you, do you?

No!

You don't want it to be dormant and stagnant, do you?

No! I want to use it for God's glory. I want to live my life by it!

Great. How are you going to do that?

Oh. Wow. I don't know.

The way you live by His power—the way you reach inside and grab that power and splash it on your lifestyle—is by staying plugged into the power source.

And…

And that means reading your Bible consistently and praying consistently. That's part of the secret, remember?

Oh, yeah!

But that's not all.

There's more?

Ab-so-tute-a-lootly.

What?

Now that you're living in the secret—and now that you've tapped into the secret power—there's more special power available to you!

How can there be more? What other power than the power of the Holy Spirit is there?

It's the power of the gifts He wants to give you.

I get gifts?

Yep. And that's the next part of the power secret. Not only do you get His secret power—you also get special powers in the form of unique and incredible gifts from Him to you!

WOW! This is too cool! I get secret powers in the form of special gifts. YES! And it's not even Christmas!

When you discover your special powers through the special gifts He wants to give you, it's like having Christmas every day of the year!

So how do I get them? How can I find out what they are?

That's the next step in this exciting journey! But before we continue our hike, I want you to meet a special 15-year-old girl who has the gift of evangelism. It took her a while to discover what her gift was. And it may take you a while, too. In fact, you may be tempted to look at the negative things in your life and think, *I can't see anything good in all of this. There's no way I even have a gift.*

God gives each of His children a gift. And He uses the good things as well as the bad things in our lives to help us discover what our gift is.

Sad Beginning...
Happy Ending

10

The Nightmare

Imagine you're a Chinese girl living in a small village in Burma.

Your mom dies when you're six years old, leaving you to live with your grandmother and your stepdad—and he's addicted to opium. When you're 10, a Chinese woman wanders into your village recruiting young girls for prostitution.

To support his drug habit, your stepdad sells you for a lousy $100, and you're taken almost 1,000 miles away to a brothel—a place where prostitutes sell their bodies for sex—in Bangkok, Thailand.

You're only 10, and you're scared to death. Since you're from a far-away village, you don't understand the Thai language. The men who purchase you for a night of illicit behavior are mean. They beat you and ask you to do despicable things.

The owner of the brothel keeps you locked in a room. Alone. In the dark. You miss your grandmother and everything familiar. Escape? It's impossible. The door is locked from the outside.

For Maey (pronounced Ma-WEE), who's now 15, this nightmare was real. But because we serve a God who is powerful enough to make good things happen out of anything, her story is now a positive one.

I met Maey on a trip to Thailand with Compassion International. She melted my heart with her warm smile.

Here's the rest of her story, translated from her own words.

Passage to Patpong

There were 80 women and girls at this particular brothel who were being sold as prostitutes. We were in a section of downtown Bangkok called Patpong, one of the most prominent places in the world for preteen and teen prostitution. There are even travel agencies in Europe and Asia that advertise "sex tours" to this red-light district. Approximately 4,000 prostitutes work this four-block area.

I was held captive in this brothel for three months. The police finally raided the place. I was scared to death. Two officers broke through the locked door of my room in the middle of the night. I didn't understand what was happening—just that I had to go with them. I wasn't even allowed to grab any of my belongings.

I was taken to jail and questioned. The police later took me to a children's shelter. I lived there for two years, mopping floors and doing all kinds of scrub work.

The staff at the children's shelter heard about an organization called the New Life Center. The center ministers to prostitutes and has a live-in facility for those who don't have a home and don't want to return to prostitution.

The children's center staff told me there were girls there who spoke my language, so when asked if I'd like to live at the New Life Center in Chiang Mai (about an eight-hour drive from Bangkok), I accepted.

An assistant housemother began reading the Bible to me, starting in Genesis. She encouraged me to attend a nearby church that preached in my language. I was fascinated. I'd never heard of such a God who could love me so unconditionally.

Most of Thailand is Buddhist, but I came out of a different upbringing. I was an animist. That means I was taught to believe that spirits were in everything and everywhere. So the whole idea of Christianity, forgiveness, and heaven was all brand-new to me.

After I had gone to church for a few Sundays, the pastor announced that in two weeks he would baptize anyone who wanted to give his or her life to God, but he needed to know by the following Sunday if any of us wanted to be included.

I left the service and immediately began praying to a God I'd never spoken to. "Are You real, Jesus? Is becoming a Christian the right thing to do?" It was all so confusing.

Each night I was plagued with horrifying nightmares. Demonic spirits danced around me screeching, "If you become a Christian, we'll kill you. Don't trust Jesus; He's a liar."

I wanted so badly to accept Christianity, but these demonic forces were all I had ever known. I knew they could hurt me and even make me sick, so I didn't want to make them mad. But I continued to think about everything the pastor had said and wondered if there could actually be a God so kind. On Saturday night I had another dream. This was completely different from the nightmares of previous nights.

I saw a beautiful green field with a cross in the center. As I walked toward it, the demons told me to leave and that I was in great danger. But I felt such peace, and as I neared the cross, I noticed Christ's body. A bright light illuminated Him—a light so radiant I thought for sure I'd be blinded.

Of course, when I woke up I wasn't blind, and I knew then that I wanted to become a Christian. "Lord," I prayed, "I want to follow You the rest of my life. Please forgive my sins."

The next day I practically ran to church. It felt so good to enter my name on the list of those who wanted to be baptized and commit their lives to Jesus.

A week later, I prayed with my pastor and asked God to make me a brand-new person. He forgave me of the bitterness I had harbored for years against my stepfather. Jesus became the replacement for the family I didn't have, and as I was being baptized, I felt cleansed from

the inside out.

That evening, a demonic spirit approached me again. His face was contorted, and I'll never forget the words he hissed. "I have no power to come and bother you anymore because you've given your life to Jesus Christ," he said. "You are now a child of God."

The demons have never come back, and God has done tremendous healing in my life. I used to be extremely frightened of men. I'm not anymore. God has assured me that whatever man does to my body, it cannot affect my soul. God's in charge. He owns me now.

+ + + + + + + + + + + + + + + + + + +

Maey still lives at the New Life Center with several other teen girls. She just finished the ninth grade, and her favorite subjects are Thai and English. She plans to continue her schooling and eventually wants to attend Bible school and become an evangelist. Since learning the secret of life in Christ and living in His Supernatural power, Maey has discovered God has gifted her with a genuine passion for those around her.

She aches for others to know God as she knows Him. Her deepest desire is to bring people into a personal, growing relationship with Jesus Christ. She's developing the gift of evangelism that God has placed within her.

Here's what I'm thinking about after reading this chapter...

What Are the Gifts?

Maey has the gift of evangelism, but she still has to develop it.

Again, God wants to bless you with a gift, but you may need to work to develop that gift to its full potential.

Imagine someone who has a wonderful physique and is very muscular. He has a great desire to be a long-distance runner; but without training, discipline, and work, the ability will never grow. The athlete needs to learn how to pace himself. He needs to develop his gift. The muscles are there. The desire is there. But he has a responsibility to do his part—develop the gift with the help of a coach.

Think of the Holy Spirit as your spiritual coach. He may have already placed a specific desire within you and could be molding this desire into your special gift. But you still have a responsibility. You have to unwrap the gift before you can use it. That's where your spiritual coach comes in. The Holy Spirit will help you discover and unwrap your gift. And as you discipline yourself to Him daily, He'll coach you in how to develop your gift to bring glory to God.

STEP 8

Know what gifts are available. It's tough to discover your special power wrapped inside a gift if you don't know what the gifts are. That's like trying to bake a cake without knowing which ingredients to use. So this next step in our journey is to take a quick peek at the packages—the gifts God gives.

Spiritual Gifts and Their Definitions

All of the gifts were designed by God to help His people—the Body of Christ—work together. As you read through the following definitions, think of some ways that pairs or groups of these gifts could be used together, resulting in a more effective ministry than if just one of them was used alone.

Apostle: The gift of apostle is the special ability God gives certain members of the Body of Christ to assume and exercise general leadership over a number of churches. This person has extraordinary authority in spiritual matters. His or her authority is credible because of the fruit produced by the ministry. (People can easily recognize God working through this life in this specific way.) This is spontaneously recognized and appreciated by those churches.

Missionary: The gift of missionary is the special ability to minister in a second culture.

Evangelism: The gift of an evangelist is the special ability God gives to certain members of the Body of Christ to share the Good News (the gospel) with unbelievers in such a way that men and women become Jesus' disciples and responsible members of the Body of Christ.

Prophecy: The gift of prophecy is the special ability God gives to certain members of the Body of Christ to receive and communicate an immediate message of God to His people through a divinely anointed utterance.

Pastor/Teacher: The gift of Pastor/Teacher is the special ability God gives to certain members of the Body of Christ to assume a long-time responsibility for the spiritual welfare of a group of believers.

Exhortation: The gift of exhortation is the special ability God gives certain members of the Body of Christ to minister words of comfort, consolation, encouragement, and counsel to other members of the body in such a way that they feel helped and healed.

Knowledge: This gift is the special ability God gives to

certain members of the Body of Christ to discover, accumulate, analyze, and clarify information and ideas that are pertinent to the growth and well-being of the Body of Christ, the church.

Wisdom: The gift of wisdom is the special ability God gives to certain members of the Body of Christ to know the mind of the Holy Spirit in such a way as to receive insight into how given knowledge may best be applied to specific needs arising in the Body of Christ.

Teaching: The gift of teaching is the special ability God gives to certain members of the Body of Christ to communicate information relevant to the health and ministry of the body and its members in such a way that others will learn.

Music: A person with this gift enjoys glorifying God through the medium of singing and/or instrumental praise.

Craftsmanship: A person with this gift enjoys using their hands to create, build, draft, or produce something that will glorify God and His people.

Helping Gifts

These next eight gifts best exhibit the presence of the fruit of the Spirit in the life of the Christian. When a person uses these gifts, it indicates spiritual maturity and consecration more than the use of any of the other gifts.

Administration: The gift of administration is the special ability God gives to certain members of the Body of Christ to understand clearly the immediate and long-range goals of a particular unit of the Body of Christ and to devise and execute plans for the accomplishment of these goals.

Giving: The gift of giving is the special ability God gives to certain members of the Body of Christ to contribute their material, physical, mental, or spiritual resources to the work of the Lord with generosity and cheerfulness.

Helps: The gift of helps is the special ability God gives to certain members of the body of Christ to invest their talents in the life and ministry of other members of the

body. This enables the person helped to increase the effectiveness of his or her own spiritual gifts.

Serving: The gift of serving is the special ability God gives to certain members of the Body of Christ to identify the unmet needs involved in a task related to God's work, and to make use of available resources to meet those needs and help accomplish the desired goals.

Hospitality: The gift of hospitality is given to some members of the Body of Christ to provide an open house and a warm welcome to those in need of food and lodging.

Leadership: The gift of leadership is the special ability God gives to certain members of the Body of Christ to set goals, in accordance with God's purpose for the future, and to communicate these goals to others in such a way that they voluntarily and harmoniously work together to accomplish those goals for the glory of God.

Mercy: The gift of mercy is the special ability God gives to certain members of the Body of Christ to feel genuine empathy and compassion for individuals, both Christian and non-Christian, who suffer distressing physical, mental, or emotional problems, and to translate that compassion into cheerfully done deeds which reflect Christ's love and alleviate the suffering.

Discernment: The gift of discerning of spirits is the special ability God gives to certain members of the Body of Christ to know with assurance whether certain behavior that's *said* to be of God is in reality divine, human, or Satanic.

Special Effects Gifts
These cause the most excitement and misunderstanding within the church. Because of their flamboyancy, they are often desired and are given wrong priority among Christians. These gifts can lead to carnality, selfish use, and misuse. Discipline, scriptural teaching, and spiritual leadership are needed to direct these gifts. These gifts are needed to increase the levels of expectancy within the church body.

Faith: The gift of faith is the special ability God gives to certain members of the Body of Christ to discern with

extraordinary confidence the will and purpose of God for the future of His work, to declare it, and to act upon it.

Miracles: The gift of miracles is the special ability God gives to certain members of the Body of Christ to serve as human intermediaries through whom it pleases God to perform powerful acts that are perceived by observers to have altered the ordinary course of nature.

Healing: The gift of healing is the special ability God gives to certain members of the Body of Christ to serve as human channels through whom it pleases God to cure illness and restore health apart from the use of natural means.

Tongues: The gift of tongues is the special ability God gives to certain members of the Body of Christ to praise Him in a nonexistent language (prayer language) or in a real language not known to the one speaking it.

Interpretation: The gift of interpretation is the special ability God gives to certain members of the Body of Christ to make known a message of one who speaks in tongues.

Intercession: The gift of intercession is the special ability God gives to certain members of the Body of Christ to pray for extended periods of time on a regular basis and see frequent and specific answers to their prayers to a degree much greater than that which is expected of the average Christian.

Martyrdom: The gift of martyrdom is the special ability God gives to certain members of the Body of Christ to undergo suffering for the faith—even to the point of death—while consistently displaying a joyous and victorious attitude which brings glory to God.

Celibacy: The gift of celibacy is the special ability God gives to certain members of the Body of Christ to remain single and enjoy it; to be unmarried and not suffer any undue sexual temptation.

Exorcism: The gift of exorcism is the special ability God gives to certain members of the body of Christ to cast out demons and evil spirits.

The Fruit of the Spirit

You already know the Holy Spirit has special powers He wants to give you through a unique gift.

But did you also know the Holy Spirit has some incredible fruit He wants to cultivate in your life?

I've heard the term "fruit of the Spirit," but I've never really understood it.

Before we chat about how to discover your secret power through your special gift, let's talk about the fruit of the Spirit first. God may only give you one or two gifts, but He wants you to have *all* of the fruit the Holy Spirit produces; and there are nine different fruits that can be cultivated in your life.

What are they?

Great question. And as always, we can get our answer from the Bible—our source of absolute Truth.

"But the fruit of the Spirit is love, joy, peace, patience, kindness, goodness, faithfulness, gentleness and self-control" (Galatians 5:22-23 *NIV*).

Let's have some fun with this. Grab your gel pen and take a few minutes to create a clever bumper sticker slogan for each fruit. Here's an example:

Have LOVE, will show it!

Your turn. Fill in each of the blank bumper stickers below with your own creations.

Now try to match each fruit with its correct definition. (I'll provide the answers upside down at the bottom of the page.)

1. **Love**

2. **Joy**

3. **Peace**

4. **Patience**

5. **Kindness**

6. **Goodness**

7. **Faithfulness**

8. **Gentleness**

9. **Self-control**

A. Excellence of character; the quality or state of being good.

B. Control over one's own impulses, emotions, or acts.

C. Bearing pains or trials calmly.

D. To hold dear; cherish; strong affection and devotion.

E. Mild; delicate.

F. Doing good and bringing happiness to others.

G. Tranquility.

H. Great happiness; gladness.

I. Steadfast in keeping promises or performing duties.

Keep your gel pen out! Read the following scenarios and see if you can guess which fruit of the Spirit each girl is expressing.

1. When Kellie meets Shannon, the new girl at school, she offers to show her around and eat lunch with her. Which spiritual fruit is Kellie demonstrating?

_____

2. Hannah finds out that Ericka has been spreading lies about her and ruining her good reputation. She's really hurt, but she's also angry. "Ugh! How could she do this to me?" Hannah says to her friend Jennifer.

_____

1. D 2. H 3. G 4. C 5. F 6. A 7. I 8. E 9. B

"Go tell her off!" Jennifer says.

"I want to," Hannah replies. "Believe me; I really want to! But I'm not going to because I know it's not the right thing to do."

Which spiritual fruit is blossoming in Hannah's life?

_____

3. The first-grade Sunday school teacher called in sick at the last minute and the children are out of control.

"Jessica, would you mind substituting in this class?" Pastor Evans asks.

"Sure, I'll be glad to," she responds.

Jennifer's friend Haley tagged along to help but was soon frustrated beyond words at the boisterous and energetic children. Jennifer remained calm and gathered them in a circle. She told a Bible story and calmly engaged the kids in a friendly discussion about the different characters of the story.

"Wow, Jennifer!" Haley said. "You never lost your cool. That was amazing."

Which spiritual fruit was oozing through Jennifer's actions?

_____

4. For Annie, visiting Uncle Frank's farm with her family was the highlight of the summer months. He had sheep, goats, dogs, cows, and horses. One afternoon, several lambs got loose and scattered throughout the hills. Uncle Frank asked his son, Kevin, to bring them back to the pen.

"I'll go with you," Annie said. "Maybe I can help."

Once Kevin and Annie located the baby sheep, Kevin frantically ran in circles and screamed at the animals to follow him.

Annie approached the frightened animals and talked

softly to them, eventually pulling, pushing, and coaxing them back to a general area where they could be herded to the pen together.

Then she noticed one little sheep was limping. Annie sat on the ground and held the baby in her arms. Very carefully, she pulled the thorn from its foot, while speaking to it in soft tones.

"Wow, Annie! If I didn't know you, I'd think you'd lived in the country all your life," Kevin said. "That was incredible. You were so careful with each one! I think I've learned a few things from you today!"

What spiritual fruit was Annie displaying with the sheep?

_____

5. Ryan couldn't help but notice Rachel. In fact, everyone noticed her. She was like a magnet. People seemed to be drawn to her. She had a great laugh, and she was always smiling.

One day he said to her, "Rachel, you're really a happy person, aren't you? I mean, even when things don't go so great, you always have a cheerful attitude. That's really cool!"

Which fruit of the spirit had Ryan noticed in Rachel's life?

_____

Remember, you won't have every spiritual gift available, but you *can* have all of the fruit of the Spirit! You don't have to choose. God's desire is for you to demonstrate every single one of them through your lifestyle.

How do I do that?

We can take our clue from their name: fruit of the *Spirit.* That tells us that the Holy Spirit can develop each fruit in

your life. In other words, you can't "will" it on your own. And you won't simply wake up one morning and be full of patience and peace. It's a developmental process; it takes time.

But surrendering your will to the Lordship of Christ is the beginning.

I've done that.

Yes, you have. So you're already on the right track. And as you continue to grow closer to Christ (reading your Bible, praying, fellowshipping with other Christians, finding a ministry in your church or youth group where you can serve), the Holy Spirit will begin developing the fruit in your life. But there *is* something that can block or hinder the growth of your fruit.

What's that?

Something called "acts of the sinful nature."

Whoa. You just lost me.

Let's take a look at what the Bible has to say about it. I think it will help you understand.

"The acts of the sinful nature are obvious: sexual immorality, impurity and debauchery; idolatry and witchcraft; hatred, discord, jealousy, fits of rage, selfish ambition, dissensions, factions and envy; drunkenness, orgies, and the like" (Galatians 5:19-21 *NIV*).

I'm still not sure I understand.

Let's look at the same verse from *The Living Bible*, which states it a little differently. Same meaning, just different words.

> But when you follow your own wrong inclinations your lives will produce these evil results: impure thoughts, eagerness for lustful pleasure, idolatry, spiritism [encouraging the activity of demons], hatred and fighting, jealousy and anger, constant effort to get the best for yourself, complaints and criticisms, the feeling that everyone else is wrong except those in your

own little group—and there will be wrong doc-
trine, envy, murder, drunkenness, wild parties,
and all that sort of thing. (Galatians 5:19-21)

Take a look at the first sentence: "When you follow your
own wrong inclinations your lives will produce these evil
results." In other words, when you do your own thing, call
your own shots, demand your own way, cling to your
rights—you'll experience the opposite of the fruit of the
Spirit. You'll experience the evil results mentioned in the
above verse.

But I surrendered my rights to God, remember?

Yes! And because of that, the Holy Spirit will begin pro-
ducing that terrific fruit in your life. But, even though
you've surrendered everything to God, there may be
times in your life when you tend to "take back" something. When that happens, the Holy Spirit will work
through your conscience and your heart to "check" you,
so you'll realize you need to re-commit that specific area
of your life back to the Lord.

For instance, let's imagine your history teacher accuses
you of cheating on a test. You really *didn't* cheat; it's a
false accusation. You've given your rights to God,
remember? So the godly response would be to talk with
your teacher in a calm manner and tell her you're a
Christian—not a cheater—and that you'd be glad to
retake the test to prove your innocence. If she doesn't
back down on her accusation, you bring your parents in
and the three of you calmly talk with her.

But let's say you don't react in a godly manner. Let's say
you storm into her room after school and scream, "How
dare you accuse me of cheating! That's so stupid! I
studied for that test for an entire hour. I didn't need to
cheat! Are you blind?"

You're now displaying one of the "acts of the sinful
nature"—anger. And whenever you display an "act of the
sinful nature" or "your own wrong inclination," you cancel
out a fruit of the Spirit. If you're displaying anger it's

likely you're not displaying love. Anger tends to cancel out love.

Let's take another situation. Elizabeth, the most popular girl in school, invites you to a party at her house on Friday night. You know she's not a Christian and you also know there will probably be things going on that you shouldn't do. The excitement heightens when Elizabeth announces, "And my parents are gonna be out of town. Everyone's coming, and we'll have the entire place to ourselves. We can do whatever we want!"

You want to go because Elizabeth is popular and it would be fun to be with the most popular kids on Friday night. But you feel "checked." (That's the Holy Spirit working through your conscience and your heart.) Deep inside, you know you shouldn't go.

But you do. And sure enough, all kinds of things are going on at Elizabeth's party that you know are wrong. Someone brings out some beer. Someone else lights up a cigarette. You don't really want any beer, but you start drinking anyway, just because you want to fit in.

Remember what we just read? Drunkenness and wild parties are listed as "acts of the sinful nature" or "wrong inclinations." So if you're experiencing drunkenness and wild parties, you're immediately canceling out specific fruits of the Spirit. It would be impossible for you to display the fruit of self-control when you're drunk and involved in a wild party.

In other words...I can't have both.

Exactly.

I think I'm starting to understand.

God wants to produce the fruits of the Spirit in your life and cultivate them through your actions. And the Holy Spirit is in the process of doing that right now. But when you stop trying to live in obedience to God it stops the Holy Spirit's production of the fruit.

Okay, so if I display anger...does that mean I'm not a Christian any more?

No. It means you've temporarily failed. But God is in the business of forgiving our failure.

So what do I do if I blow it? I really WANT to live a holy life. I WANT to be obedient to Christ. I WANT my actions to reflect the fruit of the Spirit!

And God knows that. He knows your heart. Remember, because the Holy Spirit has saturated you with His supernatural power, you don't *have* to give in to temptation. In other words, even though you're tempted to lash out in anger at the teacher who falsely accuses you, you don't *have* to. You *can* stop right then—at the moment you're tempted to scream in anger—and pray, "Jesus, help me right now. I need to do the right thing. Help me to display peace instead of anger."

And you can rely on His strength to help you react in peace.

But what if I don't? What if I act too fast—without stopping to pray and ask for help?

Again, the Holy Spirit is committed to showing us what's wrong in our lives. And He'll help you see that your attitude isn't right. When He does that, you need to ask God to forgive you.

And will He?

Yes. God is always quick to forgive.

Then what?

Then accept His forgiveness and ask Him to help you not make the mistake again. If you notice you have a track record with anger, or lying, or jealousy (or some other sin), ask your parents or youth leader to help you in this specific area. They can pray for you and with you and help you through this struggle.

Wow. The fruit of the Spirit is cool stuff!

And again—the exciting thing is that you don't have to choose just one or two pieces of fruit. They're all yours!

Okay. But what does the fruit of the Spirit have to do with the secret power stuff?

A couple of things. First, when you allow the Holy Spirit to develop His fruit in your life, you're then in line to receive and develop your special power through your spiritual gift from God.

So I don't get my spiritual gift until I develop the fruit?

No, you'll still get your gift. But you won't develop it until you allow the Holy Spirit to produce His fruit in your life. Let's imagine I give you a mountain bike.

Cool!

But you don't know how to ride a bike.

Yes, I do.

This is an imaginary situation, so work with me.

Okay. I don't know how to ride a bike. (Though I can't figure out why.)

You just never learned. Anyway, I give you this brandnew, shiny blue mountain bike. The gift is yours. You have it. But you'll never *use* it until you learn to develop the skill of riding. I'll hire a bicycle coach for you. His job is to produce a bike rider out of you. If you allow him to work with you, he'll produce in you the ability to ride the bike. But the bike is yours regardless of whether or not you allow the coach to work with you.

God gives every one of His children a gift. But until you allow the Holy Spirit to produce His fruit in your life, you'll never really use your gift—just like you wouldn't use the bike.

I get it!

But there's one more reason the fruit of the Spirit is important to the special gift God wants to give you.

What's that?

I mentioned in Chapter 11 how the helping gifts (administration, giving, helps, leadership, mercy, and discernment) are the ones that best reflect the fruit of the Spirit in the life of a Christian. So, the fruit of the Spirit really go hand-in-hand with the gift God wants to give to you.

Wow. This is so cool. I never knew this before.

And now that you know what the spiritual gifts are and what the fruit of the Spirit is—and how they go together—let's discover what your gift is!

YES!!!

Here's what I'm thinking about after reading this chapter...

What's Your Gift?

Hey, I gotta pause for a second and just let you know how proud I am that you've read this far!

You're doing super! And God is smiling from ear to ear because you're learning about the secret power He has in store for you.

Discovering your spiritual gift is an exciting process. But let's take a few minutes to recap, okay?

You learned way back at the beginning of this book that tapping into the secret power requires following a series of steps. Fill in the missing words in each step. (It's okay to flip back a few pages if you can't remember.)

Step 1: _____

Step 2: _____

Step 3: Read the _____

Step 4: Go to _____

Step 5: Develop a strong _____

Step 6: Know what really _____

Step 7: Access the power of the _____

Step 8: Know what _____ are available.

Congratulations! You've made it through eight exciting steps! Ready for the next one? Here it is!

STEP 9

Discover and develop your spiritual gift. Grab your gel pen and gear up for a fun quiz that will help you figure out what your spiritual gift is.

Okay! I've got my pen.

Great. Before we use it, let's pray.

Pray?

Yes. Remember, prayer is always the route we take when we need to know something. And since you need to know what your spiritual gift is, let's pray.

That makes sense.

> *Dear Jesus:*
>
> *I don't know what my spiritual gift is, but I sure am excited to find out! Please help me as I take this quiz. I realize finding my gift may be a process; it may take a while. That's okay. I'm ready for the journey. In Your name I pray, Amen.*

Unwrapping Your Spiritual Gift

This evaluation, designed to help you identify and develop your God-given gift, is kind of long. So grab a refill on your drink before you start, okay?

For each statement, select the value from 0-4 that indicates how true the statement is when it's applied to your life.

Use the answer sheet on page 112 to record your answer for each question. Place each numerical response (from 0 to 4) next to the corresponding question number. When you're finished, combine each row of scores and then record each row's total in the "Row Total" column on page 113.

Locate your highest three scores and circle the name of the spiritual gift listed in the column to the right of each one. Then write the names of your top three scoring spiritual gifts on the lines given on page 114.

1. I enjoy working behind the scenes, taking care of little details.

2. I usually step forward and assume leadership in a group where none exists.

3. I enjoy cheerfully providing food and a place to stay for those in need.

4. I have the ability to recognize a need and get the job done, no matter how trivial the task.

5. I have the ability to organize ideas, people, and projects to reach a specific goal.

6. People often say I have good spiritual judgment.

7. I am very confident of achieving great things for the glory of God.

8. I am asked to sing or play a musical instrument at church functions.

9. Through my prayers, God has made the impossible possible.

10. I have an ability to use my hands in a creative way to design and build things.

11. I have, in the power of Jesus, cured people's illnesses.

12. I enjoy giving money to those in serious financial need.

13. I enjoy ministering to people in hospitals, prisons, or rest homes to comfort them.

14. I often have insights that offer practical solutions to difficult problems.

15. I have understood issues or problems in the church and have seen answers when others didn't.

16. I enjoy encouraging and giving counsel to those who are discouraged.

0 = Not at all

1 = Little

2 = Moderately

3 = Considerably

4 = Strongly

17. I have an ability to thoroughly study a passage of Scripture and then share it with others.

18. I presently have the responsibility for the spiritual growth of one or more young Christians.

19. Other people respect me as an authority in spiritual matters.

20. I have an ability to learn foreign languages.

21. I have ability in the area of communication and public speaking, and people enjoy listening to me.

22. I enjoy spending time with non-Christians, especially with hopes of telling them about Jesus.

23. I enjoy praying for long periods of time.

24. I would like to assist the pastor or other leaders so they will have more time to accomplish their essential and priority ministries.

25. I am often chosen as the leader in a group of people.

26. I enjoy entertaining guests and making them feel at home when they visit.

27. I enjoy serving others, no matter how simple or little the task.

28. I am a very organized person who sets goals and makes plans to reach them.

29. I am a good judge of character and can spot a spiritual phony.

30. I believe God could cause any church to grow to 10,000 people.

31. I believe I could sing well in the choir.

32. God has used me to make things happen which were far beyond human means.

33. I enjoy doing things like woodworking, crocheting, sewing, metal work, stained glass, etc.

34. I have seen God work through my prayers to heal people.

35. I joyfully give money to the church well above my tithe.

36. I feel compassion for people who are hurting and lonely, and I like to spend time with them to cheer them up.

37. God has enabled me to choose correctly between several complex options in an important decision when no one else knew what to do.

38. I enjoy studying difficult questions about God's Word, and I am able to find answers easier and quicker than others.

39. People often tell me their problems, and I encourage them.

40. When a question arises from a difficult biblical passage, I am motivated to research the answer.

41. I take an active role in protecting Christians from worldly influences that would hinder their spiritual growth and weaken their faith.

42. I would be willing and excited to start a new church.

43. I can adapt easily to a culture, language, and lifestyle other than my own, and I would like to use my adaptability to minister in foreign countries.

0 = Not at all

1 = Little

2 = Moderately

3 = Considerably

4 = Strongly

44. I will always speak up for Christian principles, even when what I say isn't popular and people think I'm narrow-minded or hard-headed.

45. I find it easy to invite a person to accept Jesus as his or her Savior.

46. I pray at least one half hour daily for other people, believing God to answer my prayers.

47. I enjoy relieving others of routine tasks so they can get special projects done.

48. I don't mind asking others to accomplish an important ministry for the church.

49. Our home is often used for parties and social activities.

50. I am very dependable for getting things done on time, and I don't need much praise and thanks.

51. I easily delegate significant responsibilities to other people.

52. I am able to distinguish between right and wrong in complex spiritual matters that other people can't seem to figure out.

53. I often step out and start projects that other people won't attempt, and the projects are usually successful.

54. I believe I could sing in the choir and be an important part of the worship service.

55. God has used me to work spectacular miracles in the lives of others.

56. I would like to make posters or decorations for church activities.

57. God has healed people because of my faith.

58. God has blessed me with the ability to make more money than I need, so I cheerfully give much to the church.

59. I want to do whatever I can for the needy people around me, even if I have to give up something.

60. People often seek my advice when they don't know what to do.

61. I have an ability to gather information from several sources to discover the answer to a question or learn more about a subject.

62. I feel a need to challenge others to better themselves, especially in their spiritual growth, without condemning them.

63. Others listen and enjoy my teaching of Scriptures.

64. I like to give of my own free time to meet others' needs.

65. Other Christians accept my spiritual advice without questioning me.

66. I would like to present the gospel in a foreign language in a country whose culture and lifestyle is different than my own.

67. I feel a need to speak God's messages from the Bible so people will know what God expects of them.

68. I try to win my friends to Jesus every chance I get.

69. I believe praying is the most important thing a Christian can do.

70. I would like to do things such as typing, filing, gardening, painting, etc. for the church—or help in any way I can.

71. I can guide and manage a group of people toward achieving a specific goal.

72. I would like to use my home to get acquainted with newcomers and visitors to the church.

73. When I see a little job that needs to be accomplished, I jump right in and get it done.

0 = Not at all

1 = Little

2 = Moderately

3 = Considerably

4 = Strongly

74. I am able to recognize gifts and abilities in others and help them find a ministry where they are effective.

75. People come to me for help in distinguishing between spiritual truth and error.

76. I trust in God's faithfulness for a bright future even when everything looks bad.

77. I enjoy singing, and people say I have a good voice.

78. God has blessed my prayers so that supernatural results have come from otherwise impossible situations.

79. I find satisfaction in meeting people's needs by making something for them.

80. I enjoy praying for God to heal those who are physically and emotionally ill.

81. I wouldn't mind lowering my standard of living to give more to the church and to others in need.

82. When I hear of other people without jobs and who can't pay their bills, I do what I can to help them.

83. God enables me to make appropriate application of biblical truth to practical situations.

84. I can recognize difficult biblical truths and principles on my own, and I enjoy this.

85. People will tell me things they won't tell anyone else, and they say I am easy to talk to.

86. I am organized in my thinking and systematic in my approach to presenting Bible lessons to a group of people.

87. I enjoy working with people and desire to help them be the best person they can be for the Lord.

88. I am accepted as a spiritual authority in other parts of the country or world.

89. I would like to share the gospel in foreign countries.

90. I find it relatively easy to apply biblical promises to present-day situations.

91. I would like to tell others how to become a Christian and give them the invitation to receive Jesus in their life.

92. The Lord has answered many of my prayers for others.

93. I enjoy helping others get their work done, and I don't need a lot of public recognition.

94. People respect my opinion and follow my direction.

95. I feel that entertaining guests in my home is a real ministry.

96. I enjoy helping people in any type of need, and I feel a sense of satisfaction in meeting that need.

97. I am comfortable making important decisions—even under pressure.

98. I can sense when a speaker is empowered by the Holy Spirit or just bringing glory to himself.

99. I often exercise my faith through prayer, and God answers my prayers in exciting ways.

100. I believe the Lord could use me in the choir to deliver a message through song.

101. God uses me to work miracles for the glory of His Kingdom.

102. People say I am gifted with my hands.

103. People often seek me out to pray for their physical healing.

104. When I give money to someone, I don't expect anything in return, and I often give anonymously.

105. I enjoy working with the unfortunate and the "have-nots" who are usually ignored by most people.

106. People usually do what I recommend and remember advice I have shared with them.

0 = Not at all

1 = Little

2 = Moderately

3 = Considerably

4 = Strongly

107. People have come under conviction from my insights of Scripture and their application to daily life.

108. I enjoy encouraging discouraged people so much that I sometimes neglect other responsibilities because I am spending so much time with them.

109. I get excited thinking about having the opportunity to share in a Sunday school class concepts and details about Scripture that are relevant to daily life.

110. I help Christians who have wandered away from the Lord find their way back to a growing relationship with Him.

111. I would be excited to share the gospel and form new groups of Christians in areas where there aren't many churches.

112. I have no racial prejudice and have sincere appreciation for people very different from myself.

113. I feel God's blessing, power, and anointing when I am publicly speaking His message.

114. I have a strong desire to help non-Christians find salvation through Jesus Christ.

115. Prayer is my favorite ministry in the church, and I spend a great deal of time at it.

1		24		47		70		93	
2		25		48		71		94	
3		26		49		72		95	
4		27		50		73		96	
5		28		51		74		97	
6		29		52		75		98	
7		30		53		76		99	
8		31		54		77		100	
9		32		55		78		101	
10		33		56		79		102	
11		34		57		80		103	
12		35		58		81		104	
13		36		59		82		105	
14		37		60		83		106	
15		38		61		84		107	
16		39		62		85		108	
17		40		63		86		109	
18		41		64		87		110	
19		42		65		88		111	
20		43		66		89		112	
21		44		67		90		113	
22		45		68		91		114	
23		46		69		92		115	

Total	Spiritual Gifts
	A. Helps
	B. Leadership
	C. Hospitality
	D. Serving
	E. Administration
	F. Discernment
	G. Faith
	H. Music
	I. Miracles
	J. Craftsmanship
	K. Healing
	L. Giving
	M. Mercy
	N. Wisdom
	O. Knowledge
	P. Exhortation
	Q. Teaching
	R. Pastor/Teacher
	S. Apostle
	T. Missionary
	U. Prophecy
	V. Evangelism
	W. Intercession

My Top 3 Spiritual Gifts

1._____

2._____

3._____

Before we wrap up this chapter, let's take a moment to pray. In the box below, write out a prayer of thanks to God for these very special gifts and ask Him to help you fully develop each of them so you can start using them to glorify Him.

Dear God: _____
_____
_____
_____
_____
_____
_____
_____
_____
_____
_____
_____
_____
_____
_____
_____
_____
_____

Discovery Sometimes Takes a While

14

Now that you've taken an evaluation, you might have a clearer idea of what your spiritual gift is.

Or not. What if I still don't know?

That's okay. Sometimes it takes a while to figure out what we're good at.

Whaddya mean?

Well, you may not know that you have the potential to be a dynamic speaker because you may not have had the opportunity to do any public speaking. If you've never sung in a choir or taken music lessons, you probably won't know if you have any musical skills. If you've never had the opportunity to teach a group of people, you won't know if you have the gift of teaching.

Yeah, that makes sense.

Often our desires go along with our spiritual gift. For example, if you enjoy helping others, you may have the gift of encouragement but don't know it yet. I'm a writer, but it took me a while to discover I had the gift of communication or teaching, but I knew I had an interest in this area.

How'd you know?

When I was in fifth grade, our class received the assignment to read a book, write a report, and present the report orally. I did that. And afterward, I wrote my own book and reported on that, too. I began to realize that I

enjoyed creating stories and presenting them verbally. Now I travel around the world speaking to teenagers.

It's exciting how God gives us our heart's desires when we're obedient to Him. There's nothing I enjoy more than communicating Jesus to people in a public setting. This requires that I write a message and then present it orally. I love doing this! And I have the gift of teaching. God has definitely given me my heart's desires.

You may not be absolutely sure yet what your spiritual gift is, but if you'll live in obedience to God, He'll give you your heart's desires. And usually—our desires and interests go hand-in-hand with our spiritual gift!

Mother Teresa had a unique interest in helping the poorest of the poor. God blessed her interest, equipped her with His supernatural power, and this small-boned lady raised millions of dollars to help people in great need.

Rosa Parks was interested in equality, and her courageous act of not going to the back of the bus was so supernaturally powerful that the world hasn't been the same since! Simple interest in a small thing leads to powerful changes in the world. God gives us unique interests and curiosities that can lead to powerful ministries and historical changes.

Power, Gifts, and Secrets

Got your gel pen handy? Use your Bible to answer the following questions.

1. **Read 1 Corinthians 4:1. What are we entrusted with?**

   _____

   _____

2. **Check out Mark 4:11. What secret has been given to you?**

   _____

   _____

3. Take a peek at Philippians 4:12. What special secret did the apostle Paul learn?

_____

_____

4. "For God's secret plan, now at last made known, is Christ himself. In him lie hidden all the mighty, untapped treasures of wisdom and knowledge" (Colossians 2:2-3 The Living Bible). According to this verse, what's the secret? Where can you find the treasures of wisdom and knowledge?

_____

_____

5. Read Psalm 68:34. What are you supposed to proclaim?

_____

_____

6. Take a peek at James 5:16. What is powerful in the life of a righteous person?

_____

_____

7. According to 2 Corinthians 12:9, in what is God's power made perfect?

_____

_____

8. Check out Romans 9:17. What does God want to display in you?

_____

_____

9. Flip to Colossians 2:10. Who is the head over all power?

_____

_____

10. Look at Jude 25. In whom do you have power and authority?

_____

_____

11. In your own words, write out what the "secret" is, as it's been explained in this book.

_____

_____

12. Now jot down what the secret "power" is, as it's been explained in this book.

_____

_____

A Secret Power Girl

What is a Secret Power Girl? It's someone who has accepted Jesus Christ as her Lord, has consecrated her gifts for His use, is committed to pray and read the Bible, is dedicated to allowing the Holy Spirit to produce spiritual fruit in her life, and is in the process of discovering and developing her special power through her God-given gift.

Her strong relationship with Christ gives her confidence. And because she understands that God loves her no matter what, she loves and accepts herself. People are naturally attracted to a Secret Power Girl. They admire her confidence, and they are drawn to her genuineness. They want to be around her because she truly cares about others and is confident enough to reach out to them.

Is she perfect? No. But when she blows it, she seeks God's forgiveness and learns from her mistake. She's determined to become all that God dreams for her to be.

What does she look like? Some Secret Power Girls are tall and others are short. Some are chubby and others are thin. There are Secret Power Girls who are shy and Secret Power Girls who are outgoing. Some Secret Power Girls enjoy being in front of people; others would

rather work behind the scenes.

Secret Power Girls don't have a specific look. They come in all sizes, shapes, and colors. However, they are all totally in love with Jesus Christ, and they are all living with a supernatural power that is clearly not their own. Secret Power Girls are the ones who will make a difference in this world because God will use them for His glory.

The Secret Power Girl hides God's truth in her heart and then implements that truth in her life. This truth is a secret power that non-Christians see in her actions and long to have for themselves.

Secret Power Girl on a Reservation

Eighteen-year-old Crystal White Mountain grew up in Texas. Her dad is a Sioux Indian, and her mom is a Mexican-American. Crystal tapped into the secret of a strong relationship with Christ when she was a child. After a summer vacation spent visiting her dad's family on Standing Rock Reservation in South Dakota, Crystal's parents couldn't get the reservation out of their minds.

Though they were living a comfortable life in Texas, they felt the Lord leading them to move to Standing Rock Reservation. At first, Crystal felt out of place. After all, she was city girl now living in an environment that seemed foreign. But she knew she was where God wanted her to be.

She eventually became friends with Native Americans and prayed that God would shine through her life. Her dad now pastors the church on the reservation, and Crystal is involved in a weekly children's program called KIDS' JAM, for Jesus And Me. Crystal and a friend lead the weekly Sunday night ministry together for an hour of puppets, praise and worship, Bible stories, memory verses, and games.

"There's a lot of depression on the reservation," Crystal explains. "We want to be God's light in the darkness." Many of the children and teens suffer from the effects of fetal alcohol syndrome—the name for various birth

defects that occur in infants born to women who consume large amounts of alcohol during pregnancy.

Crystal is living in a tough environment, yet because she's a Secret Power Girl, she's not afraid of the oppression that surrounds her. She's developing her God-given gift of teaching, and she's striving to be the hands and feet of her Lord to others.

Here's what I'm thinking about after reading this chapter...

Counterfeit Power

15

Even though Crystal White Mountain

(who we met in the previous chapter) knows the power of God saturating her life, she's also aware of the powers of the world such as drugs and alcohol that she sees ruining people's lives on the reservation.

God desires to give you holy power, but Satan wants to distract you with counterfeit power. He and his demons search for anything and everything to distract and destroy your self-esteem, your abilities, and your tender heart.

So you're telling me that Satan is totally out to trip me up!

Exactly. Satan is so cunning!

What's that mean?

It means he's extremely deceptive. In fact, the Bible calls him the father of lies. In other words, he's a master of deceit and evil. There are three ways he works very hard to tempt you.

1. He works overtime to make sin look good. Satan is very smart! He knows it's tougher to tempt you with sin that looks ugly and horrible. So he entices you by packaging it in glitter, allure, and passion. Someday Satan will try to tempt you into being sexually involved outside of marriage. Which tactic do you think he'll use: (A) Showing you cases of teens with incurable sexually transmitted diseases, people dying of AIDS, and teen girls who have been abused by their boyfriends? Or (B) A good-looking, muscular guy who showers you with flattery? Which of those two tactics would tempt you? Again, Satan's goal is to make sin look good.

Imagine Satan wants to tempt you to shoplift something. You know stealing is wrong. How do you think he'll tempt you? (A) By bringing images to your mind of women in

prison who were caught shoplifting? Or (B) By bringing images to your mind of you wearing that really cool necklace at the upcoming party?

It's usually not the ugly stage of sin that tempts us. We're allured into sin. And Satan is the pro at knowing how to do that.

Think about the false religions in the world today. Wicca, for instance, is considered a good religion by those who practice it. A Wiccan will tell you she uses her powers to cast good spells and that Wicca is all about honoring Mother Earth.

That may not sound so bad, but as you take a deeper look, you'll realize that Wicca is simply sugarcoated Satanism. *Any* power that's not of God is of Satan. Wiccans will deny this. "We don't even believe in Satan," they say. "We're all about doing good." Well, guess what? They're being deceived. Which brings us to Satan's second tactic.

2. He deceives you into a state of denial. Wiccans, or those who are witches, deny that Satan even exists. His greatest ploy is to deceive us into believing that there *is* no Satan. When you hear someone say they don't believe in Satan, know that Satan is laughing his head off! He's won the battle in that person's mind. Using deceit, he has led that person into a state of denial—causing them not to believe in his existence.

In the same way, once Satan has used his first tactic and lured a teen girl into becoming sexually active with her boyfriend, he'll then switch to his second tactic of denial. You may hear a friend say, "There's nothing wrong with what we're doing. We love each other! And when you're in love, it's okay to demonstrate that love through sex."

Guess what—that's denial. And it's a lie straight from Satan. God has clearly said that sexual intimacy outside of marriage is a sin. So it doesn't matter if love is in the picture or not. Sex outside of marriage has always been a sin and *will* always be a sin! Anyone who disagrees has been deceived by Satan and is in denial.

3. He uses ugly self-demeaning lies to create doubt. Though we're usually not tempted by something that's ugly and horrible, Satan knows your vulnerable (that is, weak) areas. He'll pounce on them and exaggerate the doubts you have, causing you to believe ugly lies about yourself.

For example, if you don't like the way your nose looks, Satan will use an ugly lie and entice you to believe your nose is truly horrendous and that everyone stares at it in horror. If you think you're a little overweight, he'll exaggerate that belief into an ugly lie and cause you to believe you look gross and disgusting. These harmful lies can lead to the self-killers known as eating disorders (anorexia and bulimia).

If you're feeling lonely, Satan will exaggerate that feeling and try to convince you that no one likes you, people talk about you behind your back, or you'd be better off running away.

What's the solution? Know your weak areas! And when you're being tempted with ugly lies in these specific areas, recognize that temptation is coming straight from Satan. Immediately turn to God in prayer and seek His help.

Do you know that all temptation comes from Satan? Anything that makes you want to draw closer to God is worth pursuing. But anything that causes you to doubt yourself or to go against God's will is something to stay away from because it's from the hand of Satan.

Check this out: "And remember, when someone wants to do wrong it is never God who is tempting him, for God never wants to do wrong and never tempts anyone else to do it" (James 1:13 *The Living Bible*).

Paraphrase the above verse in the space provided on the following page.

_____'s Paraphrase of James 1:13
(write your name here)

_____

_____

_____

_____

_____

_____

_____

_____

_____

_____

_____

_____

_____

_____

Now let's take a peak at James 1:14-16 from the Living Bible: "Temptation is the pull of man's own evil thoughts and wishes. These evil thoughts lead to evil actions and afterwards to the death penalty from God. So don't be misled, dear brothers." According to this verse, what do

_____

_____

_____

_____

evil thoughts lead to?

Now read the above verse again. What are we told

NOT to do?

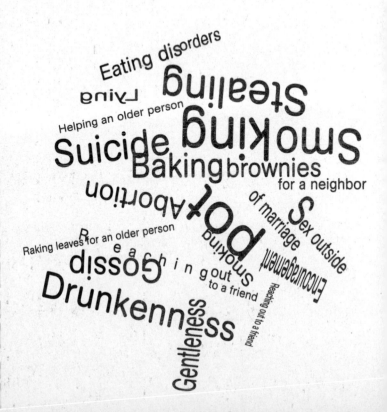

Eating disorders

Stealing

Lying

Helping an older person

Suicide Smoking

Baking brownies

for a neighbor

Abortion Pot

Raking leaves for an older person

Reaching out to a friend

Gossip Reaching out to a friend

Smoking of marriage

Sex outside

Encouragement

Drunkenness

Gentleness

God is full of good, holy, and perfect power. Satan is full of evil and wicked power. Circle all the things below that are a result of Satan's evil power.

Letter from Satan

Again, Satan will do anything to get your attention off of Christ. Don't listen to him. Keep your eyes focused on Jesus and your ears tuned in to the Holy Spirit. Now that you know what Satan's tactics for temptation are, be especially aware!

Hey, Christian!

I saw you yesterday as you climbed out of bed and started your daily routine. You looked in the mirror and I heard everything you said: "Ugh! Why am I so fat? I hate myself!"

Ha! Guess who placed those thoughts in your mind? ME. That's right; I'll do anything to get you to stop thinking about Jesus. So I've turned your attention to your body. And I laugh in glee when I hear you diss yourself. I love it! I am so glad you're becoming obsessed with stupid things that have absolutely no eternal value at all—like your weight, your hair, and your complexion.

You idiot! You have no clue what's happening, do you? Do you have any idea how much I loathe you? To say that I hate you would be a gross understatement. I loathe you! I can't stand the sight of you! You make me sick. And it's all because of Jesus. Ugh. I even hate the sound of that name.

If He didn't love you so much—if only He hadn't given His life for you—my job would be much easier. But He went to the Cross. And He did it willingly because He's in love with you. I'll never understand why He wants you of all people to spend eternity with Him.

So go ahead. Take a good long look at yourself in your bedroom mirror. Worry about your jeans. They look stupid on you. Your stomach's so fat you look horrible in anything you wear!

Uh, oh. You just ate a piece of toast. How dare you? Don't you realize how much bigger that's going to make your hips look? Do you think any guy is going to pay attention to a girl with huge hips?

You stupid idiot! Why did you eat that toast? Now you've got to get rid of it. Go ahead. Kneel in front of the toilet. Make it your throne. Insert finger in mouth.

Yes!

Ha-ha-ha. You're such a moron. I've got you throwing up and taking laxatives and thinking about every single calorie you eat. You couldn't even take communion last Sunday at church because I had you so obsessed about how many fat grams were in the bread.

Do you have any idea how much joy I get from making you miserable? My goal in life is to kill you—emotionally, spiritually, and physically.

So keep obsessing about your weight. Keep striving for physical perfection that won't mean anything at all throughout eternity. If I can take the fun out of your life—if I can keep you from being happy with the person God created you to be—if I can keep your thoughts on yourself instead of Him and His dreams for your life, I'll be laughing forever.

And I mean it.

Spitefully yours,

Satan

Here's what I'm thinking about after reading this chapter…

Deceit from the Enemy

16

Imagine holding so much hurt on the *inside* that experiencing great physical pain on the *outside* would seem minor.

Chava was 15 years old when she started hurting herself. "I had a really low self-esteem," she says, "and I was always condemning myself." In an effort to take her mind off of the deep hurt she was harboring in her heart, Chava began cutting herself and burning her arms with a curling iron.

If you have a friend who is experiencing self-mutilation, he or she may be known as a "cutter." It's dangerous and your friend may be stuck with physical scars for a lifetime.

It's difficult to understand why someone would voluntarily inflict pain on herself, isn't it? No one simply begins cutting herself for the fun of it. It's painful. The person involved in cutting is someone who has begun to believe an exaggerated lie from Satan (remember tactic number three from the previous chapter?).

Take a further peek at Chava's story and see if you can recognize the deceit from Satan.

Chava's pain happened right before she entered her

teen years. "When I was 11," she says, "my family moved to Israel. While on vacation at a beach, I was raped by a 29-year-old lifeguard."

She didn't tell anyone. She assumed the rape was her fault because he offered her a ride and she voluntarily got in the car with him. And she was embarrassed.

"I didn't know what to do with all that hurt," she continues. "It just wouldn't go away. It kept growing and gnawing at my insides."

Despite the nightmare she experienced at the beach, Chava enjoyed living in another country and learning about a different culture. "My dad is a rabbi," she says, "and my family loved being in Israel."

But when she turned 15, her dad decided to move the family back to the United States. "I didn't want to come back," Chava explains. "I became very bitter about having to move again—and having to move such a long distance. I was just getting used to the culture, the food, the climate, and the people."

Trying to Fit In

When Chava arrived back in the States, she felt like an outsider. "I spent a lot of time trying to figure out where I fit in," she remembers. "All my friends had changed. It was really hard to find common ground with anyone—even with my best friends. They all thought I was weird."

Chava eventually discovered one of her friends was bulimic. "I had always carried a phobia about my weight," she says, "and the fact that my one friend was bulimic influenced me to obsess about my own weight."

Because Chava was still hiding the pain from being raped, it didn't take long for her to attempt to fill the void in her life by controlling her weight. She began throwing up three times a day and finally got to the point where eating anything made her physically sick.

Her parents noticed the changes in their daughter and tried to help, but because Chava was determined to continue hiding her pain, they were limited in what they

could do. They *did*, however, get her into counseling.

The Hurt Won't Go Away

Not only was she dealing with the secret of being raped, weight fluctuation, and rejection from friends, but then a month after she returned from Israel, Chava's grandpa shot himself and died. "I saw him one day and he died the next," she remembers.

"I didn't want to keep thinking about all the hurt inside me. I was desperate to get my mind off all the sadness and confusion I was feeling," she says. So one day at a friend's house, when Chava was 15, she took a sewing needle and scraped her hands and arms. "Later, I told my mom that my friend's cat had scratched me," she says.

"Part of me was thinking, *I can't believe I'm doing this*. But the other part of me was someone able to numb the pain on the *inside* because now I was focusing on a different pain—a physical pain on the *outside.*"

Is There Hope?

Chava was finally hospitalized because of excessive cutting and a suicide attempt. She was diagnosed with major depression and was placed in a locked-down facility. "I felt very far from God," she remembers. "I kept thinking, *He won't love me. Why would He? I'm too unworthy. I'm worth nothing.*

But Chava's parents and church family continued to love her and pray for her. When she was released from the hospital, she began attending a weekly women's Bible study with her mom. "It was four hours long," she says. "We'd bring our workbooks and read out loud and really dig into the Scripture."

Chava had loved dancing since she was a child, and one day the Bible study group was listening to some soft music during their prayer and worship time. "The song was 'El Shaddai,'" Chava remembers. "I've always loved that song. I felt God was touching me in a special way.

During the next few minutes, I got up and danced the song for the women."

Afterward, the women surrounded Chava and prayed with her. "I gave God 100 percent," she says. "I gave Him everything! I can't go back to the hospital. I can't continue to self-destruct. I can't keep destroying the temple God has given me."

Is she still tempted? "I'll be honest," Chava says. "I still struggle with the temptation to cut myself. I'm still battling bulimia, but God is working with me. Some of my healing may take time, but He's not giving up on me. I've surrendered myself to His care, and with His help, I know I'll make it.

"I'm so much closer now to my parents," Chava says. "The biggest help they've given me is to make me realize they're not giving up on me. They hug me a lot. They smile with their eyes as well as their mouth, and they show me in a million ways that they love me.

"My parents bought me a journal and assured me that it was for all my private thoughts and that no one would ever read it unless I chose to share it. There's such a security in that. So, I'm writing down my thoughts now," she says. "That really clears my head. I love to write poetry.

"Later, I go back and re-read what I've written and it helps me gain a clearer perspective of what I'm struggling with. I also try to listen to calming music. Some of my favorites are: Twila Paris, Kim Hill, Nicole Nordeman, and Point of Grace."

+ + + + + + + + + + + + + + + + + +

The Lies

Did you catch the deceit Satan used to tempt Chava into being destructive? He began by trying to convince her that being sexually abused (raped) was somehow her fault. He built on that lie and made her feel guilty and embarrassed. (If you, or a friend, have been sexually abused, it is *not* your fault! Sexual abuse is a crime and

should be reported immediately to your parents and the authorities!)

When Chava returned to the States, Satan fed her the lie that she didn't fit in. He exaggerated the lie to deceive her into thinking no one cared about her; no one wanted to be her friend.

Since she had gained a little weight, Satan jumped on that weak area in her life and exaggerated that, too. He made her feel she was unattractive, fat, and unlovable. That particular lie led to an eating disorder. And as Chava began to believe more and more of Satan's lies, she began cutting herself.

What do you think Satan was doing the entire time Chava was hurting? He was laughing his head off! Aren't you glad God doesn't give up on His children? He continued to love Chava and brought the right people into her life until she finally gave her heart to Christ and tapped into the secret of His power. She no longer believes the lies of Satan because she now knows the Truth. She's a Secret Power Girl on the road to discovering her God-given gifts to use for His glory.

Secret Power Girls
Are Overcomers

Saying it's what's on the inside that counts in one thing—believing it and living it are another.

Only Secret Power Girls are the ones who can truly do this! Meet Nann Chafin—a teen girl who stopped by the office of *Brio* magazine to meet with the staff and share her story.

+ + + + + + + + + + + + + + + + + + + +

"Ugh! I'm having such a *bad* hair day!"

Remember mumbling these words under your breath as you headed to school last week—and the countless times you repeated them as you stood in front of the bathroom mirror with your friends, desperately doing whatever you could to remedy the horrible situation surrounding your head?

Most of us have had days when we've been less than thrilled with our uncooperative hair. *Some* of us have gone so far as to consider chopping it all off. But not *all* of us.

Eighteen-year-old Nann Chafin is one girl who's not complaining about her hair. That's because since she was 12, Nann hasn't had much hair to complain about. Within a few months of her hairstylist first discovering a

dime-sized bald spot on the back of her head, Nann went from a full head of thick, blond curls to a head with a few strands of hair here and there.

Upon noticing the initial bald spot in August 1993, Nann's hairstylist said it looked like *alopecia areata*, an auto-immune deficiency, and suggested that she visit a dermatologist. Nann's mom called a doctor from the salon, and after a consultation the dermatologist confirmed that Nann had *alopecia areata*.

The Scoop on Alopecia

So what does it mean to have an auto-immune deficiency that makes your hair fall out? Simply, it means that Nann's immune system thinks she's allergic to her own hair. There are different varieties of *alopecia*. Nann has *totalis*—it affects only her head. People who have *universalis alopecia* lose all their hair—eyebrows, eyelashes, leg hair, etc. Others who have less severe cases resulting in a patch of missing head hair or arm hair may not even realize they have *alopecia*. Because *alopecia* is so rare, and because it is not life-threatening, the government hasn't allocated much money to research the condition. No one knows how or why a person may have it. And without much research, there haven't been any great strides made in finding a helpful treatment or cure.

Though Nann says she wasn't worried about the first bald spot even when it grew to the size of a silver dollar, her dermatologist must have been. She immediately gave Nann more than 30 different medications to take at the same time.

"I became really weak from all the steroids, and I blew up like a balloon," Nann says.

Even though she's no longer taking all the medication, Nann still has a lot of pain in her joints. She expects she'll have some type of arthritis for the rest of her life.

More Than a Bad Hair Day

By January 1994, Nann's head was covered with bald

spots. As her hair began to thin, she accumulated a collection of hats and got permission to wear them to her public school.

"For a long time I had a little bit of hair on the side of my head," Nann explains. "I could tease that and curl it and make it look like I had a little bit more hair than I did.

"I wore hats, but kids can be cruel. I remember this guy came up and jerked my hat off. People were standing around, and then all of a sudden they just stopped and stared. It was like they didn't know if they should do something, or if they should laugh. Some *did* laugh.

"I said to this guy, 'Are you finished?' He snickered and tried to be cool. So I said, 'Can I have my hat back, please?' He reluctantly returned it, and I put it back on. I said goodbye and walked down the stairs.

"It was the end of the school day, and I went home and told my mom, 'I'm not going back.' She woke me up the next morning for school, and I said, 'Mom, I'm not going back.' She said, 'Okay, we'll get the necessary papers to school you at home.' "

In Search of One True Friend

Before Nann opted for home schooling, she was involved with several activities at her school. Even while she was dealing with the effects of *alopecia* and the medications she was taking, she didn't let her pain keep her from making worthwhile contributions.

When Nann realized there wasn't a student choir at her school, she recruited an interested teacher and students and went before the school board and principal to request a choir. Today the school has a chorus program and Nann is invited to come back for concerts.

Nann says students thought a lot of her—when she had a full head of hair. Instead of having just *one* group of friends, she was in *every* group. During lunch she'd often move from able to table to visit with as many people as possible.

But once she started losing her hair, Nann began losing "friends" too.

"I used to have a seat saved for me all the time at lunch," she remembers. "Once I started losing my hair and wearing hats to school, I'd walk up and there'd be no seats.

"When I'd sit down, people would literally get up and move. Even when we'd be walking somewhere, everyone would get in this huddle with their backs to me and leave me completely out.

"I basically had the same people in all my classes, and they didn't talk to me anymore. Whenever I'd put my fingers through my hair or put it behind my shoulder to lean down, I'd have to shake hair off. People complained about getting hair on their desk. When something like this happens, you really find out who your true friends are."

As if classes and lunch time being unbearable wasn't enough, Nann had to put up with insensitivity from teens during other parts of the school day as well.

"Girls would go into the bathroom after lunch to brush their hair and freshen up for the rest of the day. When *I* did that, it was just embarrassing," she says.

"I wouldn't try to brush my hair, but I'd wait for other girls to do theirs. They'd said, 'Oh, I *hate* my hair! It never does anything right. I'd stand there thinking, *If you only knew…*"

Looking for the Bright Side

When Nann finally decided she'd had enough of public school, her dermatologist reluctantly signed her homebound papers. She hesitated because she thought Nann needed to get on with her life and be out in public. To Nann's dermatologist, dealing with *alopecia* seemed like no big deal. She didn't understand the middle-school world Nann was living in that put so much importance on a person's outer appearance.

Once Nann was away from daily contact with other teens, she realized just how much she depended on God. "I know God helped me through everything," she says.

"It's been hard to explain because it's so personal—
between God and me. I finally figured out that He
helped me one day at a time. Sometimes for an hour at
a time. He helped me little by little.

I never, *never* let go of God. I never doubted Him. But
sometimes I'd get frustrated. Sometimes I'd think, *I know
what I don't have...I don't have my hair, I don't have my
friends at school, I don't even have school anymore.*

"One day, I decided to sit down and think of what I *did*
have. I thought and I thought. Finally I just said, 'I've got
God. That's what I've got. I've got God, and my youth
group, and my family.'

"What in the world would I do if I let go of God? What
would I have? I'd have just this negative, nothing. I'd
probably be in a fetal position on the floor somewhere,
all depressed. Thank God that He didn't let *me* let go of
Him."

While Nann is highly involved in her youth group, she
says she still goes for days without getting one phone
call from a friend. Sometimes she thinks friends in her
church don't realize that they're even more valuable to
her now since she doesn't have connections with teens
at school anymore.

"I'd love to have friends call and tell me what happened at
school, or have them ask about my day at home school,"
she says. "Sometimes the support just isn't there. It still
comes down to one or two. God, and one or two people."

Firm Foundation

Once during a service at church, Nann went to the altar
for prayer. "I told my pastor, 'I want you to pray for my
alopecia.' He started praying for me, but the entire prayer
was for my 'Aunt Patricia.' I was laughing, and he thought
I was crying and was patting my back."

Along with prayer, whether for her *alopecia* or non-exis-
tent Aunt Patricia, Nann has gained much of her strength
through Scripture. Paraphrasing Psalm 46, Nann says, "I
love how it says, Nations will rise up against you and

mountains will crumble, and all of a sudden He says, 'Be still, and know that I am God.' When it gets to that part, peace comes over me. Just be still, and know that I am God, and I am here. That's all I need to know.

"I just read somewhere that faith is neither sight, nor sense, nor reason, but just simply believing in God. Just believe in God. Faith the size of a mustard seed can move mountains, so if just believing in God can move mountains, think what can happen if you believe that God can perform miracles!"

She's Back!

Before Nann left South Carolina to visit the *Brio* staff in Colorado, she said something to her youth pastor that blew him away. "When I come back," she said, "I might stop wearing my wig."

When Nann showed up in *Brio* land, she was without the wig, but wore a purple scarf wrapped around her head. It matched her sweater perfectly. A few weeks after we met Nann, her mom wrote to fill us in on how Nann was doing. Here's an excerpt from her letter.

"I must give you this update on Nann. Her interview has inspired and strengthened her. When we returned home, she found the courage to go before her youth group and share a little of what she's been through. She then told of her desire to not wear her wig anymore around them. Many of them didn't even know she wore a wig.

"With tears streaming down her face, Nann said, 'I'm not wearing my wig anymore, and I need to know it's all right with all of you.' Sobbing, she reached up and slowly, deliberately, took off her hair in front of more than 50 teens and adults.

"That night, with the strength from God through the encouragement of her interview with *Brio*, Nann was free from bondage—after five years we feel our Nann is back. She's bruised and broken, but brave, strong and once again flashing that huge smile with freedom behind it.

"Sometimes God chooses not to physically heal, but He

always heals in His own way and chooses our paths for His glory!"

+ + + + + + + + + + + + + + + +

If you'd like more information about *alopecia areata*, write to the National Alopecia Areata Foundation at P.O. Box 150760, San Rafael, CA 94915-0760.

Knowledge from Nann

With all that Nann's experienced in going from a sought-after beauty pageant contestant to a teen without hair, you'd expect that she's learned something about life. Well, she has. Here are some thoughts she has to share with you.

Acceptance:

"I've learned that people can accept somebody in a wheelchair, or somebody without an arm, but when I come in without hair, it's like 'Oh, she looks sooo sick. What's wrong with her? Better not get too close.'

"Some people let go of their friendship with me. I think that they finally got too frustrated trying to understand what was going on in my life. They didn't just accept it.

"When you meet someone who's going through a battle, just accept it and be a friend. I'd much rather have people come up to me and say, 'How'd you lose your hair,' than just stare or give me funny looks."

Beauty:

"The things of this world absolutely do not matter. I've been in beauty pageants. In fact, the Miss America Pageant contacted me many times asking me to represent South Carolina. I never responded.

"We put so much focus on appearances. I've won first place in talent competitions and was so active in school, but when it comes right down to where the rubber hits the road, all that matters is faith in God."

Challenges:

"God has placed every situation and every detail of everything that you go through there for a reason. One day He'll place something in your life, and you'll think, *This is why God has given me this*. And it will be worth every bit of the struggle.

"For me, that time is when I give my testimony and people come up to me and say, 'God sent you here just for me.' The first time I gave my testimony, a lady leaned over behind me and said in my ear, 'I've been contemplating suicide, and you changed my mind completely.'

"Of course, that was God through me, but when she said that, I was thinking, *It's worth everything then, I've saved a life! God saved a life through me*."

Update on Nann

Since meeting Nann a few years ago, a lot of exciting things have happened in her life! She has received numerous invitations for speaking engagements and enjoys sharing her testimony wherever God opens a door. She has even become the spokesperson for the National Alopecia Areata Foundation!

Nann's going without her wig every day now. Well, almost every day—she *does* put it on occasionally for fun. Nann completed her senior year of high school at a local Christian school and graduated with 60 in her class.

Even though she has had many exciting opportunities in the past couple of years, she's experienced some difficult times, too. A few months ago, she spent time in the hospital battling mono-hepatitis with pneumonia. Nann has since been involved in mission trips and international travel and is pursuing a local cable television ministry as she continues to share her testimony.

+ + + + + + + + + + + + + + + + + +

I'm excited that Nann is able to maintain such a positive attitude while struggling with a disease that affects her

personal appearance. The key, of course, is the fact that she has tapped into the secret of a strong, intimate personal relationship with Christ. Nann is discovering her special power through her God-given gifts of communication, teaching and kindness and is using them to bring glory back to Him.

(This story was originally printed in the September 1998 issue of Brio *magazine and was written by Marty McCormack. Used with permission of* Focus on the Family.*)*

Here's what I'm thinking about after reading this chapter...

_____

_____

_____

_____

_____

_____

_____

_____

_____

_____

_____

_____

_____

_____

_____

_____

_____

Living It Out

Secret Power Girls aren't afraid to live out their relationship with Christ.

They're excited about using their God-given special gifts with those around them. They're willing to go the extra mile and put forth more effort to be the hands and feet of Jesus. Take the following quiz and see if you can identify the true Secret Power Girl in each case. (The following choices are not good vs. bad but good vs. better.)

QuickQuiz

1. Your dad just lost his job.

_____ Hillary says, "I'll pray for you," but then forgets to.

_____ Natalie brings a bucket of the Colonel's chicken to your house around 5 p.m.

2. You took a mean fall at basketball practice and broke your ankle.

_____ Natalie brings your homework and study guides by your house after school and offers to help you catch up during the next week.

_____ Hillary calls and says, "If you need anything, let me know, OK?"

3. Your dad got a new job in another city. Your family doesn't know anyone. Naturally, you're a little nervous during your first day as the new kid in school.

_____ Hillary sits across from you in math class

and says, "We've got a great youth group. Bible study is tomorrow night at 7 p.m. Hope to see you there!"

_____Natalie sits across from you in history. "Can I pick you up for Bible study tomorrow night?"

4. You bombed the science quiz.

_____Natalie says, "You'll bring your grade up. I'll help you study for next week's test, okay?"

_____Hillary says, "Better luck next time."

5. You lost the necklace your grandmother gave you for Christmas. It's your favorite piece of jewelry and you're devastated.

_____Hillary says, "We have a great lost and found here at school. You should check there. Maybe someone turned it in."

_____Natalie says, "Let's retrace your steps. I'll help you look for it. If we don't find it, we'll check the lost and found and ask the principal to make an announcement."

Both Christians genuinely cared, didn't they? But Natalie's efforts were always backed with *action*. Words are important, but actions are remembered a lot longer. Secret Power Girls are young ladies with action. They don't just talk about being Jesus to those around them—they do it!

As a Secret Power Girl, jot down what your response should be in the following case studies:

1. You notice a student at your school that is two years younger than you. She's sitting in a wheelchair and struggling to open the door to the gym. What's a Secret Power Girl to do?

_____

_____

2. Abbie has told you she wants to run for class president. You agree to be her campaign manager. You've heard her practice her campaign speech, and you know she's lying. When she asks, "Whatcha think?" what should your response be?

_____

_____

3. Jackie confides in you that her parents have been arguing a lot. Last night her dad stayed with relatives. She's afraid her folks may be heading toward a divorce. You're a Secret Power Girl. What can you do to help?

_____

_____

_____

4. Your friend Alisha is saying unkind—but true—things about Deidra. You and Deidra really aren't friends. Deidra spread some lies about *you* in the past and you're still hurting from them. But you've become a Secret Power Girl since that happened. How will you respond now?

_____

_____

_____

5. Your birthday is a week before Christmas. Your friends and family throw a big surprise party for you with cake, ice cream, and your favorite munchies. Every day of the following week leading up to Christmas break, there are special Christmas treats available in all of your classes. Once you're on break, your mom makes all kinds of holiday goodies, and of course, several scrumptious meals. By the time the New Year rolls in, you notice you've gained five pounds. You're tempted to think, *Gross! I'm so fat. Everyone will notice.* As a Secret Power Girl, can you recognize who this exaggerated lie is coming from? And how will you respond?

_____
_____
_____
_____
_____

6. Your best friend is ignoring you and it really hurts. Someone offers you a little marijuana after school. "It'll help you forget how lousy you feel," she says. As a Secret Power Girl, what's your comeback?

_____
_____
_____
_____
_____

God's Power: Your Power

As a Secret Power Girl, you're committed to living out your faith. At times this will be easier than others. When you're at church camp, in a Bible study, or doing something fun with your youth group, it will be easy to exercise your secret powers from your God-given gifts. But when you're surrounded by non-Christians, when you're away from home, or when you're lonely, it may be more difficult to remember that you're a Secret Power Girl.

During the tough times, stop and reflect on God's power—since that's where your power is coming from. No matter how tough your situation is—God's power is always stronger.

Never (as in never ever ever *EVER*) underestimate the power of your Heavenly Father!

* He made a donkey talk. (Read the whole story in Numbers 22)

* He invented colors, rhyme, the Grand Canyon, and Niagara Falls.

* He knows how the tide is born and where the waves are stored.

* He gives great gifts! (Take peace, for instance: "I am leaving you with a gift—peace of mind and heart! And the peace I give isn't fragile like the peace the world gives. So don't be troubled or afraid" (John 14:27 *The Living Bible*).)

* He can make a human being from a teeny tiny sperm and a teeny tiny egg. What's even more amazing is the fact that it all started with a dirt clod! (Genesis 2:4-7)

* He knows the exact number of hairs on you head. (Matthew 10:29-31 or Luke 12:6-8)

* He can make a hyena laugh.

* His fruit wears well. (Love, joy, peace, patience, kindness, goodness, faithfulness, gentleness, and self-control. Again, for more information on this fruit, see Galatians 5:22-23.)

* He calls the stars by name...in galaxies mankind hasn't even discovered yet. (Psalm 147:3-5)

* He saw you way back when you were being conceived! (Psalm 139:13-14)

* He has your fingerprints memorized.

* He created the hop and spring in the legs of kangaroos.

* He knows the path to the distribution point of light.

* He determines how far the waves roll and with what strength.

* He's the author of intuition and instinct.

* He understands the wild in each animal He created to live on Earth.

* He tells daylight how far to spread her wings of illumination.

* He balances the clouds with exact perfection and skill.

* He used music to knock down walls! (Joshua 6)

* Though you don't deserve it, He's crazy with love for you.

* He offered a fish buffet for thousands...from one small sack lunch. (Matthew 14:13-21 or Mark 6:30-44)

Do you think it's a problem for Him to supply you with all the power you need during the tough moments of your life? (If you're tempted to say yes, think again!)

Check this out: "I pray that you will begin to understand how incredibly great his power is to help those who believe him. It is that same mighty power that raised Christ from the dead and seated him in the place of honor at God's right hand in heaven, far, far above any other king or ruler or dictator or leader" (Ephesians 1:19 *The Living Bible*).

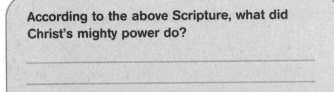

According to the above Scripture, what did Christ's mighty power do?

_____

_____

_____

For those who believe Him, what promise does His power hold?

_____

_____

_____

How great is the power of God compared to all other people in positions of authority?

_____

_____

_____

Let's take a peek at another power verse: "Now glory be to God who by his mighty power at work within us is able to do far more than we would ever dare to ask or even dream of—infinitely beyond our highest prayers, desires, thoughts, or hopes" (Ephesians 3:20 *The Living Bible*).

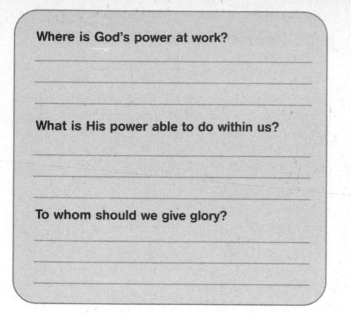

Where is God's power at work?

_____

_____

_____

What is His power able to do within us?

_____

_____

_____

To whom should we give glory?

_____

_____

_____

Staying Connected to His Power

We chatted in Chapter 8 about plugging into God's power source as an electrical cord plugs into an outlet. For you to *maintain* your Secret Power Girl status, it's important that you remain connected to His mighty power!

How do I do that?

Great question. You need to saturate yourself with things of the Lord! Here are some ideas:

✱ Memorize Scripture. Here's a good one to start with: "We are pressed on every side by troubles, but not crushed and broken. We are perplexed because we don't know why things happen as they do, but we don't give up and quit. We are hunted down, but God never abandons us. We get knocked down, but we get up again and keep going" (2 Corinthians 4:8-9 *The Living Bible*).

★ **Listen to Christian music**. No matter what is your favorite style of secular music, you can find the very same sound in Christian music. The difference? The words, Girlfriend, the words.

★ **Get a Bible** you're proud of and one that you understand. With all the student Bibles available on the market today, there's NO EXCUSE for not having one you're crazy about.

★ **Find a good teen devotional book.** No, not to replace the Bible. God's Word is the ultimate devotional book. We GOTTA read it every day to stay in tune with Him. But it's also fun to read a devotional book alongside your Bible. Why not read a short devotion in the morning and read your Bible in the evening (or vice-versa). If you're looking for a good devotional book, I wrote one called *One Year Devotions for Teens* (Tyndale Publishing). I'd love for you to read it. You can order it through any Christian bookstore.

★ **Read Christian material.** There are gobs of great Christian fiction books, romance novels, and mysteries available now. Take a trip to your local Christian bookstore and do some browsing. If you're interested in receiving a Christian magazine for teen girls, you can check out *Brio* (published by Focus on the Family). For a free sample copy, call 1-800-232-6459.

Why is it so important to saturate myself with Christian stuff?

Again, it helps you stay connected—or plugged into—God's mighty power. But it also helps you live the holy life God desires for all His Secret Power Girls. Have you ever heard the phrase "garbage in = garbage out"? It's true that whatever we put into our minds will eventually come out through our lifestyle. Whatever is on the inside

will sooner or later show up on the outside.

Check out what Proverbs 4:23 says: "Be careful how you think; your life is shaped by your thoughts" (*Good News Bible*).

What influences your thoughts? The movies you see, the TV shows you watch, the music you listen to, the conversations you soak up.

Jesus tells us that we'll know a tree by its fruit. In other words, a cherry tree will never produce apples. Likewise, one who continually cusses, cheats, gossips, and goes too far with a boyfriend or girlfriend obviously isn't displaying the fruit of the Spirit. Mature Christians grow good fruit: kindness, goodness, love, and a bunch more. (Flip back to Chapter 12 if you need a refresher course of the fruit available to you.)

What kind of fruit do others see in *your* life? Hmmm. Guess that's determined by what kind of STUFF you're allowing into your mind.

Be careful. Be really really really careful!

*Here's what I'm thinking about after
reading this chapter…*

Questions and Answers

Q: When I prayed the prayer at the beginning of the book and tapped into the secret of having a relationship with God, it felt really good. But I'm afraid I won't always feel this good. Then what?

A: Great point! And guess what—you won't always feel this good. Stuff happens in life. You'll get hurt. Someone will disappoint you. A loved one may die. Some days will just be yucky.

That doesn't mean you're no longer a Christian. You won't always feel God's presence. That's okay. The Christian life is based on faith—not feeling. You accepted Christ as your personal Savior on faith. It's great that you felt good, but even if you hadn't felt a thing, He still would have answered your prayer and forgiven your sins.

Think about this: You don't always feel the sun, do you? Some days you can't even see the sun! Do you doubt its existence just because you can't feel it or see it? No. You have faith it's still there.

Your relationship with Christ is like the sun. You may not always feel Him; sometimes you won't hear Him; but in faith you'll continue to serve Him, love Him, and believe He's with you. Check this out: "Be sure of this—that I am with you always, even to the end of the world" (Matthew 28:20 *The Living Bible*).

Q: We've talked about the special gift God has for each of us, and I'm kind of embarrassed to ask this, but here goes: What if I don't like the gift He gives me?

A: Try to remember that your desires and your gifts usually go hand-in-hand. See, God is the One who placed the desires in your heart. So if you have a burning desire to communicate Christ through music, guess who gave you that desire? And when God gives a desire, He fulfills it by complementing it with a gift.

Q: In this book we talk about the Secret Power we can get from having a tight relationship with God, but what about other secret powers—you know—like Harry Potter?

A: Remember that any power not of God is power of Satan. It may seem like harmless power and even come masked as good power, but if it's not of God, Satan is the one behind it.

Even though Harry Potter is a good kid who claims to have good powers he doesn't have a personal relationship with Jesus Christ, does he? Therefore, where do his powers come from? (I hope you know the answer to this: They come from Satan.)

I know you may not like this answer because you may have read the books or seen the movies and maybe you've enjoyed the fictional story of Harry and his friends. But remember, even though the storyline is make-believe, the occultic power on which it's based is real and Satan is the father of the occult.

Q: A lot of my friends are always talking about how they want special powers like Harry Potter. What should I say to them?

A: A survey given to 1,781 people asked what super powers they desired. Here's what they said:

* 32 percent wanted to read minds.

* 21 percent wanted to fly.

* 19 percent wanted to become invisible.

* 11 percent wanted to be indestructible.

* 9 percent wanted superhuman strength.

* 5 percent wanted X-ray vision.

* 3 percent wanted super speed.

Now that's a great list, but it's all very selfish. Look at the list again. It's all about me—what I want and how I can become more powerful for my own good. God desires us to stop thinking about ourselves and start focusing on others. That's what Jesus did. When He walked the earth, He was constantly in tune with meeting the needs of those around Him. The Bible never gives us one conversation where Jesus said something like, "Wow, I'm really tired of all these people. I need a vacation." Or "Ugh! If one more person asks Me to heal him…" Jesus loved people and enjoyed meeting their needs. God wants us to be imitators of Jesus. (For proof, check out Ephesians 5:1.)

Another interesting thing about the list is that none of them are possible to have. But here's the exciting news! There are some supernatural powers that are available to every young girl, and these powers are from God. They are available and valuable if a young girl will discover them, develop them, and use them to live the life God has planned for her. A life of power, abundance, and purpose awaits any girl who will join this adventure into the supernatural journey of being a Secret Power Girl.

So what should you say to your friends? Tell them the power they're seeking is fantasy. It's not real. Then tell them there is a power that is not only real, but also incredible beyond our imagination. Tell them you're plugged into this power and they can be, too. Then give them this book to read.

Q: Earlier in this book, you mentioned how being sexually involved with a boyfriend is a trick from Satan. My mom says sex is a powerful thing and many girls are tempted by it.

A: Your mom is a wise woman! She's telling you the truth. When you commit to remaining sexually pure until marriage, you possess a unique power of purity that most females in this world don't have.

So maybe we should chat briefly about what sexual purity is. You've probably heard that God doesn't want Christians to have sexual intercourse outside of marriage. That's true. But sexual purity goes a lot further than the act of intercourse. Sexual purity is a lifestyle! And it really does take the supernatural power of the Holy Spirit working within you to help you maintain a life of purity.

Sexual purity involves everything we watch on TV and in movies—even the music we listen to. Think about it: If you're watching a movie where two people are making love, it puts thoughts in your mind that aren't pure. If you're listening to music about people being sexually intimate outside of marriage, your thoughts are geared to go that direction.

God's plan for your thoughts is exactly the opposite: "Finally, brothers, whatever is true, whatever is noble, whatever is right, whatever is pure, whatever is lovely, whatever is admirable—if anything is excellent or praiseworthy—think about such things" (Philippians 4:8 *NIV*).

Again, sexual purity is not simply refraining from the act of intercourse. Sexual purity involves refraining from sexual intimacy outside of marriage. God wants Secret Power Girls to stand up strong for sexual purity. When you're in love with a guy and you're tempted to become sexually intimate, it may not feel good to deny yourself at that moment, but it's the right thing to do! Later you'll feel good about yourself and you'll feel empowered. Purity clears out the world's influence and fertilizes God's growth plans for you and your spiritual powers. When you possess the power of purity, your lifestyle shouts volumes to a watching world!

Q: I want to learn about more Secret Power Girls. Any ideas?

A: Yes! Check out the cool Secret Power Girls video! *Secret Power Video Devotional: Devotions Based on 5*

Christ-Following Girls Facing the Real World (Youth Specialties 2003). You'll love it, and you'll want to show it to all the girls in your youth group. It has a fun Bible study discussion guide that goes along with it, so you and your friends can have a great time doing the Secret Power Girl thing together!

Are you familiar with Dayna Curry and Heather Mercer? They're two young ladies who were imprisoned in Afghanistan for sharing their faith with Muslims. Wow! Talk about Secret Power Girls—Heather and Dayna definitely fit the description. They've written an exciting book you'll want to read. It's called *Prisoners of Hope: The Story of Our Captivity and Freedom in Afghanistan*.

You can also ask your pastor to recommend books written about female missionaries. He may have one or two in his study or there may be some in your church library. These women are definitely Secret Power Girls! Their stories will inspire and challenge you to a deeper relationship with Christ.

Calling All
Secret Power Girls!

Guess what, girls! God can use US to change the world!

It's true. Think what He did with just 12 ordinary men. Jesus chose 12 guys—some with dirt under their finger-nails, some with crooked teeth, some with ego prob-lems—filled them with His power, and sent them out to change the world.

Yeah, but they were the disciples!

They were disciples who were ordinary people! They were just like you! We could have bumped into them around any corner or seen one of them drop his lunch tray in a crowded cafeteria line.

That DOES sound like me!

But because they were filled with and transformed by the power of the Holy Spirit, they changed the world.

Good news! God wants to do the same thing with you and your Secret Power Sisses! Wouldn't it be incredible if during the next few years, girls all around the world began to discover just how many powers God has given them? That would make an amazing difference on this planet!

Girls, be excited and honored that God created you as a woman. He has always had special plans for women. Let's take a quick trip through history.

Secret Power Girls in the Bible

Mary: *The mother of Jesus.* God used this Secret Power Girl—who was quite ordinary by the world's standards—to give birth to the Savior of the world! Mary knew the secret power of living in obedience to God. Her name

will never be forgotten around the world. (Matthew 1:18-25; Mark 16:1-8; John 19:25-27; and Acts 1:12-14)

Phoebe: *She delivered the book of Romans to the people of Rome.* The apostle Paul used this single young lady to accomplish a great task. He trusted her with a powerful piece of writing—the book of Romans. Because Phoebe was willing to use her secret God-given powers, she delivered a piece of writing that's still transforming lives today! (Romans 16:1-2)

Dorcas: *Woman of encouragement.* Dorcas didn't sit on the sidelines and watch things happen. She was very involved in the early church. She used her secret power of encouragement to affirm new believers and help them grow stronger in their faith. (Acts 9:36-42)

Miriam: *Saved the life of Moses.* She risked her life to place Moses in a basket and hide him by the water's edge. She used her secret power of courage to free a future leader of the Israelites. (Exodus 2:1-10)

Esther: *Risked her life to save her people.* She became known as Queen Esther and used her secret power of influence to save the Jews from being killed. (The book of Esther)

Ruth: *She took unusual risks and discovered God's love through a godly husband.* Using her special power of generosity and faithfulness, she remained loyal to her mother-in-law after her first husband's death. God rewarded her with a wealthy second husband who cared for her as though she were a queen. (The book of Ruth)

Martha: *Had the privilege of watching Jesus Christ raise her brother Lazarus from the dead.* She used her secret power of hospitality and organization to minister to Christ Himself. (John 11:1-44)

The Widow with Two Coins: *She surrendered herself completely to God's authority and trusted Him to meet her needs.* Though known as a poor woman—and without a husband to provide for her—she used her secret power of giving to help build the church. (Mark 12:41-44 or Luke 21:1-4)

Salome: *The mother of James and John, two of the disciples. She witnessed first-hand the angel at the tomb of Jesus and heard him proclaim that Christ had risen.* She used her secret power of faithfulness and stood with others at the Cross to witness the crucifixion of Jesus. (Mark 15:37-41, 16:1-8)

Leah: *She bore Jacob six sons and one daughter.* Though she wasn't known for physical beauty, Leah used her secret power of love to be a good wife and mother. (Genesis 30:19-20)

Hagar: *She was abducted from her homeland and became a slave in another country where she was mistreated for years.* Even though her life was filled with hardship, Hagar used her special power of cheerfulness and learned that God cared intimately about her and helped her through her suffering. (Genesis 16:1-16)

Sarah: *When she was 90 years old, she gave birth to Isaac.* Sarah was part of a direct miracle from God—giving birth at such an old age—and being the helpmate and wife of Abraham—God's chosen one to father a nation. She used her secret power of courage, she was known for not giving in to fear and intimidation. (Genesis 17:15-22, 21:1-7)

The Syrophoenician Woman: *Her child was demon-possessed.* She used her secret power of faith and saw Jesus answer her prayer by freeing her child. (Mark 7:24-30)

Mary of Bethany: *She is the sister of Martha and Lazarus.* She used her secret power of faithfulness to sit at Jesus' feet and learn what He wanted to teach her. She remained intently focused on Him and refused to be distracted by the daily details of life. (Matthew 26:6-13; Mark 14:3-9; Luke 10:38-42; John 11:1-44, 12:1-8)

Mary Magdalene: *She is thought to be the first witness of Christ's resurrection.* She used her secret power of giving to pour costly perfume on the feet of Jesus. (Mark 15:37-41, 16:1-11; Luke 7:36-50; Luke 8:1-3; John 20:1-18)

Priscilla: *She was a missionary and leader of the early church.* Priscilla used her secret powers of administration and serving to spread the gospel and help the early

church grow numerically and spiritually. (Acts 18:1-3, 18-19, 24-26; Romans 16:3-4; 1 Corinthians 16:19-20; 2 Timothy 4:19)

It's Your Turn

Guess what, Secret Power Girls! Your name should also be on this list of fame. There are several more women in the Bible—and some who are still alive in our world today—whose names would also be included on the list if we had the space to record them all in this book.

Make it your goal to become a Secret Power Girl whose name is worthy of being on such a list of godly female heroes from throughout history. For the Secret Power Girl who chooses to live her life in radical obedience to the Lordship of Jesus Christ, God will turn her goal of "making the list" into a reality!

S.P. Girls, God has a special place in His heart for women. Again, throughout the course of history, God has involved women in miracles, given them special knowledge and intuition, and used them to do important things to bring about incredible changes.

Let's take a look at the amazing changes that have occurred—just in the United States—because women dared to take a stand. Not all the women were Christians or advanced Christian causes. But just look at what can be achieved when a self-assured woman steps out!

The Timeline

1862: The Homestead Act promises 160 acres of free land to anyone who lives on it for five years. Many single women "prove up claims," especially teachers who work the land in the summer and teach school in the winter.

1862: Mary Jane Patterson is the first African-American woman to receive a full baccalaureate degree from Oberlin College.

1865: Hundreds of white women go south to teach former slaves at Freedmen Schools.

1866: The American Equal Rights Association is founded—the first organization in the U.S. to advocate national women's suffrage.

1869: Iowa is the first state to admit a female attorney, Arabella Mansfield, to its bar (a professional association of lawyers).

1870: Women serve on juries in the Wyoming Territory.

1872: Congress passes a law to give women federal employees equal pay for equal work.

1875: Through her last will and testament, Sophia Smith is the first woman to found and endow a women's college. Smith College was chartered in 1871 and opened in 1875.

1877: Helen Magill is the first woman to receive a Ph.D. from a U.S. school—a doctorate in Greek from Boston University.

1879: Belva Lockwood is the first woman lawyer admitted to practice before the U.S. Supreme Court.

1883: Mary Hoyt earns the top score on the first civil service exam and becomes the first woman appointed under this new merit system. She starts out as a clerk in a treasury department.

1899: National Consumers League is formed with Florence Kelley as its president. The League organizes women to use their power as consumers to push for better working conditions and protective laws for women workers.

1910: The number of women attending college has increased 150 percent since 1900.

1917: Jeannette Rankin of Montana becomes the first woman elected to the U.S. Congress.

1920: Female college undergraduates have doubled in number since 1910.

1920: On August 26, the 19th Amendment to the Constitution is ratified, guaranteeing American women citizens the right to vote.

1926: Bertha Knight Landes is the first woman elected mayor of a sizable U.S. city (Seattle).

1932: Hattie Wyatt Caraway is the first woman elected to U.S. Senate. She represents Arkansas for three terms.

1933: Frances Perkins, the first woman in a Presidential cabinet, serves as Secretary of Labor during the entire Roosevelt presidency.

1957: The number of women and men voting is approximately equal for the first time.

1964: Patsy Mink is the first Asian-American woman elected to the U.S. Congress.

1964: Discrimination against women in the workplace is banned.

1968: Shirley Chisholm is the first Black woman elected to the U.S. congress.

1971: Cheryl Frank and Jacqueline Flenner founded the first battered women's shelter in the U.S. located in Urbana, Illinois. By 1979, more than 250 shelters are operating.

1972: Congress extends the Equal Pay Act to include executive, administrative, and professional personnel.

1972: Title IX of the Education Amendments becomes a federal law. It was written to help put a stop to sex discrimination in extracurricular programs such as athletics, band, and drama at all federally funded educational institutions.

1973: The Civil Service Commission eliminates height and weight requirements that have discriminated against women applying for police, park service, and fire-fighting jobs.

1974: Women's athletic programs receive equal funding.

1976: U.S. military academies open admissions to women.

1978: For the first time in history, more women than men enter colleges.

1990: The number of African-American women in elective office has increased from 131 in 1970 to 1,950 in 1990.

1992: Women-owned businesses employ more workers in the United States than the Fortune 500 companies do worldwide.

1992: Women win all five of the gold medals won by Americans during the Winter Olympics: Bonnie Blair—speed skating (500meters and 1000meters); Kristi Yamaguchi—figure skating; Donna Weinbrecht—freestyle skiing; and Cathy Turner—short track speed skating (500meters).

1993: Take Our Daughters to Work Day debuts. It was designed to build girls' self-esteem and open their eyes to a variety of career possibilities for women.

1996: The women on the U.S. Olympic team saw spectacular success in the Summer Olympics (gold medals in 19 events, 10 silver, and 9 bronze), a result that can largely be attributed to the growing numbers of girls and women who are active in sports since the passage of Title IX in 1972.

Your Challenge

Who knows what the years 2005, 2010, and 2015 will hold? God can use Secret Power Girls as powerful instruments to help change the world! And the exciting thing is—you can start right now! You don't have to wait until you've graduated from high school or are enrolled in college or have a family of your own to be used by Him!

Start using your secret power *now—wherever you are!* When you're baby-sitting, use your secret power of creativity to keep children entertained in a positive manner. Use your secret power of generosity and volunteer to baby-sit without pay for a single mother in your neighborhood or church.

Use your secret power of encouragement to send notes of affirmation to senior citizens, teens that have been absent from youth group, or kids who don't have many friends. Develop your secret power of kindness to create a list of random acts you can perform right now: Walking your neighbor's dog, cleaning the house for an older woman, surprising your parents with a home-cooked meal, serving hot chocolate to construction workers on a cold day, bringing treats for everyone in your class at school, telling your teacher how much you appreciate him or her. When you ask our creative God of the universe to enhance your imagination with His creativity— He'll do it!

So, Secret Power Girls, let's unite! Start praying for one another. Ask God to help you discover, develop, and use your secret powers for His glory. And let's change the world—one person at a time—beginning with you!

He _____ *nking about after*
re _____

_____

_____

_____

_____

_____

_____

_____

_____

_____

_____

_____

_____

_____

_____

_____

_____

_____

_____

_____

_____

_____

_____

_____

_____

_____